Educators Who Know

What To Do

A Collaboration with *DrCathyO*

Educators Who Know What To Do

Copyright © 2021 by Dr. Cathy Owens-Oliver.

ISBN: 978-1-7369986-2-5
Printed in the United States of America.

www.DrCathyO.com
Email: info@drcathyo.com
Phone: (980) 288 5775

Table of Contents

"Most concerned people know what they *don't* want in schools, a small number know where the re-forming of schools ought to lead us; and very few know how to get there. There are many right answers, and we are most likely to find them when teachers step into various kinds of leadership roles, share their craft knowledge, and articulate for the public and for the profession just what school and teaching might become."

Roland S. Barth

Learning by Heart

Dedication

We dedicate this book to the students who need us,

the parents who trust us, and the fellow educators

who stand with us. When we lift our voices,

we lift yours, too. We are connected.

Introduction

By Dr. Cathy Owens-Oliver

A re kids failing schools or are schools failing kids? That is the ultimate question. Given the ongoing national debate over standardized testing, common curriculum standards, teacher licensure, equity, safety, and virtual versus in-person classrooms, it is hard to tell if the learning gaps between the haves and have nots are due to a leadership issue or a teaching issue. Either way, there is a major game underway in the field of education and unless we agree on touchdown plays, we could lose the future.

We say children are the future. Do we really believe this? Does our education system prepare *all* students for the virtual, global, science-grounded, ultra-competitive society that lies ahead? The trillion-dollar edtech world has engaged effective teachers and other instructional leaders in designing an international classroom without walls while many education policymakers continue to fight over who should be the next board chairperson, how federal grants should be disseminated, and whether teachers should get paid what they deserve.

In the meantime, teachers continue to do what they do, as best they can. In this game of education, teachers are the real MVPs. They, the most valuable players on the field, know what to do when the ball is in their hands. Sadly, they get overlooked when it's time to write the playbook. They sit back and listen to all the new, grand ideas coming from the well-meaning local school board, ideas they know won't work.

It is not kosher, in most states, if teachers attend public policy meetings and speak out against the shenanigans that take place. But they don't want to be a rabble-rouser. The few who do that ultimately suffer for it one way or another. So, they sit back and wait for new policies from the district and state offices. They wait to hear the decisions they hope will not be made. They don't tell them, "This will not work and here's why." But they tell each other. Thus, these voices of master teachers, problem solvers, and game-changers seldom make it to the microphone.

They gather around televisions listening intently to government candidates, looking for the one they think will be not only the most effective, but the most honest when it comes to doing what's right for *all* kids. They watch every President's State of the Union address, listening for promises being made and praying these promises will be kept. When education officials from the state house to the schoolhouse, unveil their long-range operating plans, budget allocations, education reform initiatives, and "see-how-smart-I-am-goals," some teachers cry, some laugh, and some retire. But most resolve that "I was here when you got here; I will be here when you're gone."

After many months of watching this big game in the field on education, the continuous penalties, the unnecessary roughness, the frequent fumbles, and the landslide losses, they huddle up in the teachers' lounge to discuss why schools keep failing kids and what must be done to solve schools' biggest problems. All of them agree on one declaration: "We could've told them that; we know what to do."

We could've told them zero tolerance is a flawed policy. We could've told them educators can lead a school better than a corporate strategist can. We could've told them what won't work with common curriculum. We could've told them adequate yearly progress is skewed by various circumstances. We could've told them that high test scores don't guarantee success and low ones don't guarantee failure. But these teacher voices of the real game-changers aren't often at the table when the playbook is being designed.

The master teachers in this book, without invitation, have come off the sidelines and joined the line of scrimmage, refusing to delay the game any longer. They have innovative ideas, relevant recommendations, strategic solutions, and voices that must be heard. Given the national pandemic, most school districts are in the fourth quarter. They cannot continue with what has not worked in the past. This book puts the ball in the hands of academicians who know what to do. Make room at the table. You're about to hear from the best and the brightest.

Whether you're a parent, principal, teacher, professor, school board member or in some other education-influencing role, don't just read and listen to these experts. Suit up, take your position on the field, and let them tell you what play to run and how to get more touchdowns. These experts have been in the game a long time. Their track records and score cards speak for themselves. Follow their lead because they understand the season we are in, and they know what to do!

"When we think together, we think better and that is how we achieve what we, alone, thought we could not do."

Dr. Cathy Owens-Oliver

Sadé Wright
Elementary School Teacher

Sadé Wright is a native of Norfolk, VA and currently residing in Charlotte, NC. This is her thirteenth year of teaching with experience in second, third and fourth grade. She loves teaching scholars and helping shape the future leaders of the world. Through her time teaching, Sadé has found that fostering positive relationships with scholars is the gateway for them to achieve academic and social-emotional success. In 2007, she received her Bachelor of Science degree in Elementary Education from Old Dominion University, in Norfolk, VA. In 2019, she received her Master of Education degree in Literacy K12 from Queens University in Charlotte, NC. She is currently teaching third grade and in the process of writing her third curriculum unit for teachers. In her free time, she enjoys playing with her dog, Marley. She is a yoga novice learning different ways to relax. In the summer, she enjoys the pool and live music.

Email: sadev.wright@gmail.com
Instagram: iteach_sadew
Facebook: iteach_sadew

Personal Connections for Academic Success

By Sadé Wright

W hen was the last time your administration made you feel appreciated? When was the last time your administration showed that you mattered outside of being a teacher? How did it make you feel? Did it make you want to work harder once you realized that you mattered? Have you ever worked for an administration team that truly cared about the whole teacher? When you think about these questions, think about your classroom. What environment are you creating in your classroom for your young scholars?

In college, professors encourage teacher candidates to build relationships with scholars through the use of surveys and getting-to-know-you activities. However, when you actually start teaching, there isn't enough time for this outside of the first week of school. I've worked at schools with different philosophies for gaining knowledge of scholars. There were schools where you had the first few weeks to get to know scholars, while there were other schools where you only used the Social Studies time to get to know your scholars.

The problem we encounter with the limited-time deals with connecting with our scholars. We need more than 30 minutes or two weeks to build a solid relationship and get to know each other. As a teacher, we love our classes and scholars. However, we always have that one class every few years that pulls at our heart more than the others.

I still remember all of their names and they just graduated from high school last year. If I could have looped every year, all the way through twelfth grade, with the same class from my fourth year of teaching, then I would have. I would have switched grades and schools every year to keep that group together. When I think about why it was such a strong bond, then I think about the connection we made in the beginning.

As a fourth-year teacher, I knew the curriculum and I knew the testing expectations. Now it was time to truly learn my scholars and implement some of the out-of-the-box ideas from college. I tried different activities during instruction like role-playing and graffiti walls to learn which activities they enjoyed. A majority of them enjoyed performing. Therefore, I implemented role-playing within the Social Studies, Science, Math and Literacy curriculum. The scholars taught concepts as if they were the teacher and pretended to be characters from the book and historical figures.

I remember a moment during benchmark assessments when I overheard them talking to each other. They were telling each other how they had to do their best on the benchmark assessments to make me proud. In that moment, I knew my scholars felt the genuine love I had for them. Since the beginning of the school year, I had taken the time to get to know them and build this solid relationship.

My goal as an educator is to celebrate and honor the diverse backgrounds and traditions of learners. Through my time teaching, I found that fostering positive relationships with scholars is the gateway to the achievement of academic and social-emotional success. In order to teach a child, you have to first connect with the child. My focus is on implementing ways to build relationships with scholars early on in order to support them in the classroom and school, throughout the year.

When I use the term scholars, I am referencing active learners willing to take chances and explore. As I build relationships with scholars, they understand the importance of exploring new things and taking chances while learning. In addition, scholars understand the importance of always giving their best efforts no matter the task. Scholars are leaders in the school who set good examples for others to follow. Calling them scholars elevates their perception of themselves as learners, based on my high expectations of their performance.

The Pandemic

The pandemic has provided a broader opportunity for teachers to see the importance of intentionally building relationships with scholars and their families. Prior to the pandemic, even if a family was not involved in school, then one could still build a relationship with the scholar. During the pandemic, the need for a greater connection between home and school was heightened.

The pandemic created somewhat of a dependency between the parent, scholar, teacher and school. Teachers had to build relationships with parents who in the past may not have had the time for or interest in understanding the importance of the teacher/parent relationship. As we move past the pandemic, we need to keep the relationships strong.

Even if educators did not receive college courses or training on building relationships, the pandemic has shown us the importance of the relationship-building work needed in education. If an educator did not value relationship building, then the pandemic has given them an opportunity to see the importance and put the proper measures in place. Teaching well requires understanding the scholar, in addition to the content. It also requires a teaching and learning partnership with scholars' parents and/or guardians.

Parent Surveys and Check-Ins

Remember that parents are important. There are times when we must teach the parents how to support their children at home academically. Educators should provide parents with tools and support for effective learning at home. Past experiences may dictate current relationships. If a parent had an unpleasant experience in school, then they could transfer that experience to the relationship with the current teacher. How can we help parents feel comfortable? We can get to know the parents and guardians.

In the beginning of the school year, I call each parent or guardian to welcome them to my class. During the call, I have an opportunity to introduce myself and open the line of communication. I send home a survey where the parents give information about themselves and their child. Throughout the year, I check in with parents to update the survey and student information.

In schools, a parent can volunteer to assist the teacher with activities and events throughout the year. The parent will help with communicating events or classroom needs with other classroom parents. The parent volunteer is usually referred to as the room parent. I have taught in mostly Title 1 schools. Therefore, I rarely had room for parents to keep the other parents informed. I created a website online to update parents with information. The website can be accessed from any device. On the website, I offer tips to help scholars at home and provide practice links to websites where scholars can practice skills.

As an educator, I provide the opportunity to practice at home using approved websites instead of parents and scholars searching on their own. My website includes school announcements while featuring class celebrations. In the past, I have celebrated parent volunteers or donations with a certificate. The scholars are always so excited to receive certificates to take home to their parents. Acknowledgement is important to building a relationship. If you start the school year off by giving the parents tools, then you will gain an ally and become a team working together to ensure student learning takes place. As a teacher, we must understand that everyone wants to be heard and validated.

Family

As a teacher, you should learn as much as you can about the family of each scholar. The scholars love to share stories about playing games or spending time with their families. Most scholars light up when given the opportunity to share about their lives at home. When scholars share about their home life experiences, then educators learn more about the families' cultural beliefs, practices and diverse backgrounds. Once educators learn about this, then they can honor the family traditions within the classroom and design culturally relevant lessons.

A daily journal response question could provide students a moment to share with the class or a partner. What is your favorite place in your room and why? What is your favorite place in your home and why? Who is the funniest person in your family, and why? Describe your morning routine when you get out of bed. What do you do when you get frustrated?

The journal response question could be posted in the morning as scholars are arriving or later while scholars are packing up to leave. During transitions, scholars may think about the question and share with a neighbor. Remember, every activity does not warrant a written response. When you have scholars who struggle with writing, then you should allow them an opportunity to draw pictures or communicate verbally. There can be varying levels to the response based on the scholar's ability.

When you allow them to share, you learn more about their lives at home, you are able to identify and address concerns early on. If I know that a scholar does not have help with homework but is trying their best, then I can help the scholar figure out how to navigate the homework time. In the past, I've been informed that new siblings are being born during the school year. In some cases, the scholar needs extra support from me to help adjust to this change. By allowing scholars to share, we can understand a change in their behavior. Journal response questions unrelated to the curriculum provide insight into what is going on with scholars.

Ways to Connect

Be creative. Every child communicates differently. In the beginning, you must pay close attention to your scholars and figure out what works best for them. There are many ways to gain knowledge about scholars. This individual knowledge helps us get and keep them engaged in learning.

During my first year as a floating teacher, I worked with a teacher who made connections with her scholars by creating a weekly show. The weekly show displayed pictures and videos of her son as he was learning and exploring.

Within the past few years, I have started taking yoga classes. This year, I started a virtual yoga class where I included my dog, Marley. As Marley and I participated in the yoga class, I recorded a time-lapsed video of us. On Thursdays in class, my scholars would do a short yoga video. We would focus on learning ways to calm ourselves when we are faced with frustration and challenges.

After the yoga in class, I showed the time-lapse video of Marley and me. The scholars enjoyed seeing Marley all over the place during yoga. By sharing a part of me outside of school, I was able to make a connection with my scholars. This is not to suggest sharing everything. However, scholars need to understand that you are human just like them. Choose something interesting and appropriate to share with scholars that gives them insight from your life that will increase your rapport with them.

In the past, I have shared many of my and Marley's experiences with my scholars and they love it. In those moments, I am able to make connections with scholars who owned dogs, wanted dogs or liked dogs. Scholars with challenging behaviors seemed to shift their attitude once Marley was brought up in the conversation. By sharing a small piece of my personal life, I increased my relationship with scholars.

In my first few years of teaching, I was told not to smile until the middle of the year. I am not sure how an unfriendly teacher builds a relationship with scholars. I did not take that advice! When I was in elementary school, I would cry every year on the first day of school because I did not want to leave my mother. I couldn't imagine starting the first day of a new school year crying and seeing a teacher look at me heartless with a straight face.

I start each school year off smiling. I am excited to see the new faces. There are endless possibilities when you start the school year. Therefore, I show love to my scholars from the beginning. I laugh and joke. I want them to respect me, but I also want them to know I am just like them, only a little older. I make mistakes and I learn from them. I am not perfect. Once scholars learn that you are approachable, then you have formed a connection with them and created a safe space. When educators know a little bit more about scholars' lives and allow them to know a little about their lives, it strengthens the connections and engages the scholars. This personal connection leads to academic success.

Greeting Scholars

One of the most important expectations in my classroom is greeting others. When you walk into a room, then you greet the people in the room. We do not know what happened before a scholar reaches our door. However, once they reach our safe space in the classroom, it should feel inviting. Every scholar should be greeted when they walk into the classroom.

If you are acknowledging the scholar, then you can figure out how their morning is going. If Malachi is having a rough morning because he had an issue on the bus, then you can help acknowledge his feelings and guide him with processing his emotions. In that moment, you have shown Malachi that he is important to you. You took the time to help him solve his problem. You have given him tools to solve his problem in the future. You have built trust so that he will come to you for the next issue or concern. There are so many things to get done in the morning, but acknowledgement is the most important.

Create a Safe Space

We are together five days a week for at least seven hours over the course of 10 months. We see our scholars more in a day than we see our own families. Do you know how valuable that time in school is to our scholars? Our job as educators is to create a safe space for scholars to learn and express themselves.

In the beginning of the school year, when I ask questions about their families, I probe to see if the scholars always get along with siblings or cousins. During the conversation, we explore the family dynamic. They learn that we may not always get along or agree with our family members because there may be times when a sibling or family member is getting on our nerves. I tell my scholars, "Does that mean we don't love them? Of course not, we will always love them." After scholars understand various family dynamics, I explain how our classroom is very similar to a family. We may not always agree, but we have to protect each other and be there for each other.

Throughout the year, we read and discuss books with lessons and messages such as being honest, showing empathy and being helpful. The books help scholars make a personal connection. Incorporating books is a great way to teach lessons while creating a safe space for students to make personal connections to implement in class. Based on this use of books, my scholars have come to me about other students bullying them. We read about bullying and discuss steps to take when being bullied. During the discussion, we have a safe conversation where scholars share their experiences.

I have created a system in my classroom where scholars know they can speak to me privately about anything. It is the code of the room. I would ask them if it was an emergency or if it could wait until our next break. Afterwards, we would go to a private area in the room where other scholars could not hear our conversation. By creating a safe space, scholars knew I cared and they could confide in me.

Do you know the impact of meeting one-on-one with students? Meeting one-on-one with scholars creates a safe space in the classroom. Do you know how special a child feels when getting their teacher's undivided attention? Meetings do not have to be long and drawn out. Meeting times could take place during a transition, the morning work block, end of day while packing up, recess, or lunch. The meetings can range from discussing the weekend to sharing something they need extra help within the classroom.

The meeting is an uninterrupted time for the scholar. I use special cones to place on my desk. When the special cone is on my desk, then other scholars can only talk to me if it is an emergency. The meetings vary based on scholars' needs, but they can talk about anything. As an educator, we notice a lot with the scholars. If there is a change or concern, then the meeting times could be an opportunity to ask questions. During the meeting, you can play games, draw pictures, or answer questions. It is a special one-on-one time for scholars and teachers.

The curriculum matters, but your scholars matter even more. When scholars understand that they are more important than the lesson, then they want to learn even more. For instance, if a scholar is experiencing a meltdown or not feeling well in the middle of a lesson, will they learn anything during the lesson? No, they will miss the lesson because they are focused on their issue.

In the middle of the lesson, could you pose a quick turn and talk response question for scholars? Yes, you can use the short response time to check in with the scholar who is having an issue. You did not take away from the lesson because the response question posed added value to the lesson. In that moment, the scholar learned that you are there for him. Even in the middle of the lesson, you noticed him and made him feel valued.

All of this is important because scholars should feel safe in a classroom environment in order to learn. The cultural beliefs and practices make scholars valuable to a diverse classroom of learners. Once scholars understand their importance and uniqueness in the classroom, then learning comes naturally.

Scholar Check-ins

Are you the same person you were five months ago? Have you grown? Has your family and home life changed? Yes. And the answer is yes for our scholars, too. As we get to know our scholars, we should check in with them weekly or monthly. Think about how some months may be tougher for you based on different experiences, family issues, memories or anniversaries. This may be the case for some of our scholars. A child is a smaller version of an adult.

It is our job as educators to teach scholars how to deal with emotions daily. I express my emotions with my scholars. If I feel frustrated by certain behaviors, then I share my feelings with the scholars. By checking in with scholars periodically, we create a space where we can guide scholars through life changes and emotional challenges. This concept is critical to social and emotional learning. As an educator, you should use life experiences while teaching children how to work through their daily challenges and emotions.

As you think about building relationships and the knowledge of scholars, think about the following points.

- If someone showed you that they cared, wouldn't you do more for them?

- Your scholars are important and they need to feel important.

- The knowledge of scholars comes from building relationships with scholars.

- Scholars want to be heard just like we want to be heard.

- Create a safe space for your scholars.

- You set the tone for your classroom or school.

- Implement Restorative Practices as a means for strengthening and building classroom relationships.

- You are responsible for creating and maintaining the relationships.

As an educator, we take on many roles in our scholars' lives. In order to successfully guide and nurture them, we must first get to know them. Once we truly get to know them, we can fulfill our roles victoriously.

Gloria Sumpter
Early Childhood Specialist

Gloria J. Sumpter, a native of Bowman, South Carolina, is an Army veteran and graduate of Claflin University. She has four children and four grandchildren, all of which have been affected by her *natural teaching.* She is one of six children whose mother, with an eighth-grade education, knew first-hand the value of education gave her children many experiences. This was during the 60's, a time when children in the South were trailing behind parents working in tobacco fields. She has obtained various educational degrees related to child development: AA Psychology, BLS Liberal Studies, BS Elementary Ed, MAE School Counseling. Gloria mapped out Natural Teaching, which uses the child's environment and natural surroundings for educational discovery. She also founded the Family Success Association Inc., to be based in rural S.C. Her book, *Beneath the Fur: A Story of Acceptance, Not Tolerance,* is based on a real-life experience. Her focus is bringing parents and guardians back into the equation of educating their children and empowering them to do it well.

www.naturalteacher.org

Natural Learning Opportunities at Home

By Gloria Sumpter

T he lack of using natural learning opportunities in the home, prior to children being placed in the school system is one of the main reasons children are not well prepared for the classroom. These opportunities are missed because of guardians' lack of awareness or concern about qualifications related to their ability to teach. It is typical for some parents to feel intimidated about teaching their children at home, especially those who lack higher education.

Most rural and inner-city communities are comprised of parents with low socioeconomic status. Single parents with minimum wage income feel they lack the skills and access to prepare their children for school. All of these factors perpetuate issues of inequity and limit learning opportunities in so many communities across our nation.

Preparing Yourself for Natural Teaching

Natural teaching is defined as using the child's environment and their surroundings for teaching and learning. Not to be confused with nature-based teaching, which is bringing nature into teaching-based environments, natural teaching encompasses the MBSS: mind, body, soul, and spirit. These components make up each of us. One cannot consider being a natural teacher when one of the four is disregarded. The health of each is vital to a healthy self, home, and the natural teaching and learning experience. Before adults can be effective natural teachers, we each have some personal work to do.

This is a call for guardians to get and stay ready themselves. Being healthy (ready) in mind, body, soul, and spirit impacts the entire community. There is a paradigm regarding educating while at home that we need to shift. That is, the mindset, "My child cannot obtain it." Getting ready to teach not only at home, but in your community is vital to a permanent decrease in the dropout rate. At home, the teachers will be your family and extended family members (grandchildren, nephews, nieces, etc.), who are committed to leaving a transformable educational legacy.

But the focus needs to be extended to places like working with children in the church or community centers where you might coach or tutor. This includes involving foster and adopted guardian support and providing babysitter training and daycare provider strategies. The entire village can be helped and impacted by natural teaching. This means support in areas like training, technology, and transportation can change the paradigm so that we aren't waiting until our children are school age, where the public educational system must do all the teaching.

Again, the children are already behind if we wait. Becoming effective natural teachers in the home is the most important step to providing a strong educational foundation. This simple questionnaire about the mind, body, and soul can

28

help parents and guardians begin your path to becoming a natural teacher in your home and community.

The Mind: mental well-being, thoughts, imagination, intellect, and perceptions

1) Can I be more of an active presence than a bystander with the children in my life? (Y/N)

2) Are there areas of my mental health I know I need help with or can improve on? (Y/N)

3) Am I willing to do the daily work to get where I need to be mentally? (Y/N)

The Body: Major organs, the 11 systems, internal/external parts, and functionality

1) Do I agree I can be more actively conscious of my body? (Y/N)

2) Are there areas of my body I can improve on or need help with? (Y/N)

3) Am I willing to do the work to become closer to functioning at my highest level? (Y/N)

The Soul: Unseen energy force, the subconscious, inner self, senses, desires

1) Do I agree that my soul, however, I see it, can be improved upon for good? (Y/N)

2) Are there negative areas in my spiritual life that have not been fully processed through? (Y/N)

3) Am I willing to do the daily work to grow and expand my spiritual capacity? (Y/N)

4) Have I begun self-assessment to align my mind, body and soul? (Y/N)

To begin your mental work, consider how you think and what you think about. Using daily affirmation is a powerful tool. The first thing I do each morning, after thanking God for another day, is recite my affirmations. For example, I say, "I am loved, I am kind, I am wise, I am grateful, etc." Think as highly of others as you do of yourself. If you have fallen into the "I cant's," start now on your affirmations, using "I cans." For example, I am loved. I can love others. I am wise. I can agree that others are wise. I am smart. I can make accurate and positive life decisions.

Throughout the day, I work on my focus. How we focus and what we focus on has a direct effect on our mental stamina. It takes mental strength to balance work and life issues, especially if the issues include what is best for children. Pay attention to what you read, what you discuss, how you engage with others. Practice being fully present in meetings at work as well as conversations with family and friends.

I also make it a mental promise to others daily, to give them the benefit of the doubt, rather than judging them. Each day, I practice listening to understand first before wanting to be understood. I always use "I" remarks instead of "you" when dealing with someone, especially when the other person is argumentative. I have trained my mind to assume positive intent because we cannot put out fires with fire. These are some examples of the mental work we must do as role models for children. It takes mental stamina and focus to work with children as their little minds are easily drawn in different directions, exploring all the new wonders of life.

To begin your body work, understand that your physical body is important. Feeling mentally and or physically drained on a daily basis demands much more than a quick energy drink. It requires that one digs deep into the root(s) of the problem(s) and find daily solutions that contribute to healthy living. Maintaining and balanced, healthy body makes one capable of handling the stresses that pop up during the course of the day. Physical health requires exercise and commitment to wellness.

Try keeping a daily journal for a week. Note the times you are drained and the experiences that cause this. At the end of the week, write down ways you can improve your health. Consider things in your food (i.e., too much caffeine, fatty foods, and sodas). Evaluate your fitness activity, goals, and outcomes. Reflect upon the intentions and shifts in your spirit, soul, and mind.

One of the best strategies for becoming more active is to move about with your child during the day. Consider running outside, throwing balls, rocking your baby in your arms instead of in the automatic rocker or swing. Build forts, engage your children in yoga, walk to a nearby place instead of riding. It's easy to get active in your natural surrounding when you become intentional about it.

To begin your soul work: breathe deeply and center yourself. Know that you were born with purpose and intention. Know that you have value. The subconscious and the soul are linked together in one's thinking, even though both are mysteries we may not be truly capable of defining. It is lack of alignment between all three areas creates space for negativity and leads to depression, anxiety, and poor decision-making. Protect your children from this negative energy in the home.

To begin your spiritual work, know that spirituality is neither merit-based nor something money can buy. The Spirit realm may be defined as a connection to a higher power and driving force behind one's faith, conviction, and devotion. While it is my relationship with God that guides and defines my spiritual well-being, I recognize that everyone has their own spiritual belief system.

Spirituality is a matter of choice which is often infused with religious practices. In a traditional American education system, spirituality is usually kept separate. In a natural learning environment, both before and during early childhood education, parents and guardians decide what role spirituality plays in a child's learning.

As a natural teacher, I believe we are all spiritual beings, so we will always be searching for that part of us to be fulfilled. It is a very personal quest. It is a personal relationship, not something conjured up from intellectual or head knowledge. I wish you all the best with your spiritual journey, so you can provide the best spiritual development for your children and any other children whose lives you may influence.

The connection of MBSS to natural teaching can be associated with teaching the whole child. For parents and guardians to accomplish this fully, they must be fully healthy and willing to do the work on a daily basis. For example, if the child is always being yelled at, repeatedly scolded, or being told "no," there is a direct link to their willingness to try. But, when a child is familiar with their surroundings and is happy, learning takes place as a natural process and doesn't have to be forced.

In other words, a healthy parent (MBSS) and home produces healthy life-long learners. Everything said and done should be answered by this question. Is the mind, body, soul and spirit influencing the good of the child and with the future outcome in mind? Your habits, ways of thinking, how you speak, your behavior, and belief systems are directly affecting the young ones around you, whether intentionally or not.

The results of natural teaching and learning speak volumes about the importance of teaching children during infancy to four years old while in the home. As a homeschool mom (which is what *teaching at home* was originally called), I did not invest in the traditional school curriculum. The curriculum usually started for children, ages three or four years and was based on state regulations.

Infants through toddlers do not need structure (like what they will experience in Kindergarten) as much as they need space to explore, develop curiosity, and deepen critical thinking skills. Critical thinking involves asking questions, evaluating, and learning and then practicing thinking for themselves.

The reason natural teaching was established and should not be associated with homeschooling is because homeschooling traditionally makes up a few hours during the day with flat material. I consider textbooks and other "sit and get" materials as flat. Because the world is not flat, everything is not as simple as black and white. It is unreasonable to think toddlers would stay engaged. Natural teaching uses pop-up books, puppets, stuffed animals and other toys to draw children's attention and keep toddlers focused and engaged. Movements, diverse activities, short sentences, colors, patterns, and textures are not flat.

Reading through pop-ups with infants will stimulate the brain, as does music. Gentle massages, eye-to-eye contact and speaking to them also motivates curiosity for learning. It expands their awareness. When you are outside in the community, draw attention to shapes, sounds, colors, and textures. This helps them understand all the wonderful aspects of the outdoors and connect with the community surrounding them. As the parent or guardian, you will be able to witness their reactions.

As natural teachers, parents and guardians must help children see the world in its fullness and not flat. This includes colors, textures, shapes, sounds, aromas, letters, numbers, and much more. This means everything and everyone becomes a teaching tool. As homeschoolers, if a subject is not completed during the allotted time frame, it is considered homework. But once these assignments are completed, they are placed on shelves for the following day. In contrast, natural teaching follows the child throughout the day with engaged teaching and learning, so there is never homework. Once the day is completed, the child is off to bed.

Examples of daily natural teaching for infants look differently for a one-year-old. Infants would be greeted each morning by stimulation (i.e., rubbing the face, cheeks, and back, touching their ears, or holding their hands). This also includes calling them by name and waiting for a response. They are not only feed, clothed, burped, and returned to the crib, but talked to as they transition from waking to later being put down for a nap.

As they grow, they are introduced to the home environment (closets, refrigerator contents, bathrooms, shelves, cabinets, and other things *naturally found* in the home). They later start exploring things outside the home, such as the yard, outside play areas, the mailbox or post office, grocery stores, gas stations, stop signs, crosswalks, the library, and everything in between.

These are the *natural* environment and surroundings *natural* teachers use to teach. The implemented connections (MBSS) with the alphabet, phonics, visuals, songs, daily readings, outings, affirmations, and inside/outside activities are a part of the focus. There are countless ways to connect various facets of the home environment to a child's early learning and discovery to prepare them for not only the kindergarten experience, but the real world.

Making the areas around the home safe for exploration eliminates what I call the "dredged no." The "dredged no," is saying no to everything the child may ask for or wishes to do, instead of making safe spaces for exploration. Therefore, the parent, or natural teacher, must have an open, positive mindset and listen first to understand. Telling a child "no" without consideration of why the child is reaching for or develops an interest in something, limits learning. I encourage parents to eliminate or lessen the use of the word "no" from their vocabulary during the birth to age four years and, instead, use other fillers to replace it.

Children naturally explore things they find intriguing. This is always a learning opportunity. Their inquiry through creative thinking is a doorway to processing new information. Rather than saying "no," think of ways to explain what something is and why it must be avoided so the child will gain new information. Being creative with wording can increase a child's exploring nature or deject it. We want to heighten those natural tendencies to increase awareness of the world around the toddlers so as to promote questions and critical thinking skills.

Natural teaching is for guardians who are not placing their children in any type of daycare until the child is at least three or four years old. Guardians are anyone in the child's environment during the day providing care. They are supporters of educators and not enemies of educators. By naturally teaching children, parents or guardians can place them in public systems with confidence. First, natural teaching gives guardians back their autonomy. The thought that one has to be credentialed to teach is intimidating to some parents and guardians.

Natural teaching concepts and methods break the cycle that keeps many from taking part in their child's education. Education begins at home, not a school. Parents and guardians are the first teachers and stakeholders. They need to believe this. Thus, teachers and school administrators need to include them in the conversation. Whatever can be implemented at the early stages of parenthood needs to happen.

Second, natural teaching uses the entire community as support. The emphasis on family, community places (library, grocery store, local eateries, and places of worship) is critically important for early childhood learners. Allowing your child to interact with children and people of different cultures across these spectrums builds healthy relationships and fosters your child's development of respect for others.

When parents use words like thank you, may I, please, you're welcome, etc., it flows naturally to the child. This is when the child catches the values and interpersonal skills because they see it as a displayed practice. On a daily, language develops similarly as well. One must hear words to fully develop speaking skills.   This goes back to the whole child teaching and learning and why reading to your infant is equally important as reading to your toddler.

I highly suggest not to sit children down in front of cartoons and videos for hours unless you want them to acquire those accents and squeaky voices of Mickey Mouse, Peppa Pig, etc. Properly speaking the English language is a form of communication that children will be tested on daily. Speaking calmly, clearly, using voice inflection, and gesturing are all communication skills the child acquires, along with the skill of listening. In addition, saying short words and sentences, along with gesturing or signing, are more productive than just rambling sentence after sentence. Words like hello, goodbye, come, sit, eat, etc. are ideal first words for toddlers.

Working with my children from infants proved best practices by natural methods. I worked within the child's interest, using books as a resource during the toddler stage and a form of record keeping. We read a series and then I find the movie to watch. We watched documentaries, musicals, and movies. Music is always playing in the background: classical, instrumentals, gospel, contemporary, children's songs, and Motown on occasion.

Our home has lots of windows to count and shapes to discover. Their bedroom walls were covered with numbers, words, scriptures, alphabet, shapes, colors, and family pictures. Conversations were appropriate and grew into dinner-time discussions. My faith is the guiding factor. We live life and teach naturally alongside it.

I taught backyard Bible School during the summer and Children's Church during the year. We planted a small garden in the summer. We made ceramics during the year. We walked trails through the backwoods, made mud pies, built traps (actually caught a bird and had to take it to the vet), and made forts out of moving boxes every time the military moved us. We visited senior homes, made donations, and volunteered at shelters in the area. We visited libraries, flea markets, garage sales, antique shops, and thrift stores. We took road trips, and someone always recorded them.

My methods are easily learned by any parent and these concepts are vital to the success of family. Shifting the old paradigm of postponing education until kindergarten and letting the early childhood teacher figure out the gaps can be spurred through natural teaching. In my work with families and churches, childcare providers, new teachers and other educators, I explain how natural teaching builds healthier and stronger children, families, and communities.

Parents and guardians must not rely solely on the school system to teach children, beginning with Kindergarten. Natural learning at home is the foundation for early education. Without it, many students, especially those from high-need communities, enter traditional classrooms already behind. Early childhood teachers often cannot successfully meet the needs of every early learner because of the variance in or lack of natural teaching at home.

Natural teaching is an excellent strategy for parents or guardians of children from birth to four years old. It will make for happier, curious, critical thinkers, and the child will be able to recognize the alphabet, speak words and sentences, read, and count. Confidence and being a lifelong learner are a few of the rewards when natural teaching is implemented early and correctly.

Cassandra Cruz-Dockery
Elementary School Teacher

Cassandra is a certified Kindergarten Teacher and Team Leader, who is ready to be impactful and purposeful, outside the classroom. She has been an early childhood educator for 20+ years. She is a wife and mother of two amazing little kids. She is originally from Long Island, NY and moved to South Florida in 2012.

She created *The Blooming Scholar*, because she is passionate about educating others on the importance of supporting children in their early learning and helping them use those skills to prepare them for academic success. She supports other educators in establishing strong academic foundations for scholars, intentionally and purposefully connecting their foundational skill sets to align with academic expectation.

"When we learn together, we achieve together!"

thebloomingscholar@gmail.com
www.thebloomingscholar.com

The Little Ones Become the Big Ones!

Supporting Early Childhood Educators in Establishing
Academic Readiness
By Cassandra Cruz-Dockery

Posted on their website, John Hopkins University asserts: *"Early learning is important because it helps establish a solid educational foundation for children during their developmental years."* If the strength of our children's academic foundation begins in the early years and early learning prepares a child in becoming a well-rounded and capable adult, then why isn't the main focus on our early childhood educators and primary scholars?

I am not saying we should not give attention to the other grades, as they, too, are important. However, a consistent complaint from middle and secondary educators is that their scholars (meaning students) lack foundational skills and often are unprepared for the grade-level standards. This increases the time they are teaching basic skills rather than grade-level curriculum.

Why does this continue to happen? Because we are…

✓ Not aligning early learning to school expectations, which means we are not supporting or building a scholar's support system before they enter the school system.

41

- ✓ Not aligning what they are learning in daycare and/or Pre-K to the skills needed to enter Kindergarten successfully.

- ✓ Expecting the child to know more than is developmentally appropriate and assuming they can retain and comprehend the information.

- ✓ Packing their schedules with too many curricula and resources. Teaching random skills; coloring pages, worksheets instead of coherent content; thinking maps and comprehension skills.

- ✓ Going through the motions and merely "exposing them," rather than enriching and remediating them based on their skills level.

- ✓ Having our Pre-Kindergarten, Kindergarten, and First-grade teachers attend professional development and participate in professional learning communities, only to learn about what is occurring in the upper grades and often told to "dumb it down for the little ones."

Well, I have news for you, the little ones become the big ones! This is why supporting early childhood educators in establishing academic readiness in the primary grades is so vitally important. We need to start being intentional and purposeful in strengthening and establishing solid academic foundations beginning with educators of children ages three to eight years old.

My teaching experiences have given me the ability to help early childhood educators in connecting early learning skills with academic expectations. This includes guiding educators on how to plan rigorous standard-based lessons and how to enrich and remediate primary scholars. Supporting these educators in understanding the collection of developmentally appropriate data, conducting data chats, and aligning data to academic expectations supports the foundation of the primary scholar.

as an Early Childhood Educator (for 20+ years in Pre-K and Kindergarten), a daycare director, and mother of two, ages three and five years old, I live and breathe it! My own children entered Pre-K for the first time, during the pandemic; because I had to go back to my Title I School, where I had to teach 20 Kindergarteners virtually, traditionally, paperlessly, in person. This unexpected ordeal had my head spinning and my heart racing! I had to do something for myself, my family, my students, and my team.

This is new for all of us, educators, and students alike, because in addition to Pre-K scholars needing basic academic skills (name writing, letter identification, basic counting), they also need technology skills such as turning on and logging into a device, using the mouse, directional skills, and how to close and open applications. This is in addition to Covid-19 prevention skills, including wearing a mask all day and maintaining social distancing and personal hygiene.

It made me reflect on my first Kindergarten class in 2013, when I left my job as a daycare director in New York and moved 1800 miles south to begin a new journey as a Kindergarten teacher. I entered an unknown town and began planting my feet. My first and only elementary school found me six days into my new adventure. This would become the place where I would not only be new to the state, but new to the school and the grade. (I later became the new grade level lead!)

At this time, I only knew the Pre-K world and did not know the full expectations of the traditional school. With all my years of schooling and classroom experiences, there I was sitting in the middle of my classroom, feeling lost, overwhelmed, and misguided. I waited for so long for this moment, for my *first* Kindergarten classroom, my *first* teaching experience in a *"real school,"* and now I did not know where to start or how to set up my classroom? I was unsure what centers were supposed to look like or what the expectations were? I didn't know who to turn to for help. At that time, my grade level consisted of 100 Kindergarteners and five teachers, all of whom were expecting me to guide them.

My first set of 20 primary scholars consisted of six ESOL students—two who spoke no English, four exceptions needs students each with individual education plans, six who had attended Pre-K, two who had attended only daycare and eight who were homeschooled and/or had never attended school before. More than half had socials skills but little academic skills while others had some basic academic skills and two were reading simple sentences. What remained consistent was that we were all going to be exposed to the same standards, curriculum, and grade-level expectations.

How was I going to get all these scholars who were on various levels on the same level? How was I going to get them to learn to read, write, add, and to become independent learners and problem solvers? I know so many teachers have felt the way that I did years ago and feel the way I feel now— uncertain; but I'm trying my best to make it through in this asynchronous, synchronous, virtual, hybrid world.

As we continue teaching *post-pandemic,* we must remember that some of our students have been in their homes for over a year, learning through a device, some learning from family members, some with a strong support system, while others will not have been so lucky. Kindergarten is not what it used to be and has a completely different structure to Pre-K.

Experience has taught me to stop setting up boundaries before they happen and start creating solutions. I have learned to be a problem solver and to teach my children to become problem solvers. Problem solving at the classroom level requires early childhood educators to be intentional about instructional planning and reflective on their practices.

We need an action plan for early childhood educators and primary scholars, alike. The following are some areas for early childhood administrators, instructional coaches of primary grades, early childhood educators, daycare owners and directors can reflect on when creating an action plan.

Focus on the Foundation

We cannot continue waiting for retention years or for early learning scholars to be in danger of (or already) failing to start taking an interest in their academic development. The Early Learning Coalition states, "Early learning is crucial in helping a child become a more responsible, capable, and caring individual." Knowing this, we need to start building a connection between daycares, Pre-K and primary grades and establish a strong foundation earlier.

Education leaders must support the early childhood educator in establishing academic readiness, well before and during their Kindergarten year by aligning the skills learned in the daycares and/or Pre-K to skills needed to successfully enter Kindergarten. Being knowledgeable of a child's level of comprehension and supporting them based on their developmental levels and skills sets is absolutely crucial to their academic progress long term. Effective learning must begin in the early years.

Classroom Culture and Environment

Teachers, getting to know your students is critical to the development of the child and to the classroom culture. When you get to know your students' likes and dislikes, strengths and weaknesses, their learning styles, and developmental levels, then you can connect lessons to their interests. When you create an environment that they are a part of, it makes them feel connected to their learning.

By teaching and engaging them in your routines and expectations, ensuring that they are a part of your classroom and involved in their own academic success, will increase their engagement and involvement in their own learning. Now more than ever, our children need to be heard and spoken with, not spoken at or to! Encourage them and allow them to feel empowered when they are learning from you!

Once you have established a relationship with your scholars, your classroom culture will begin to develop. Ensure that you create and maintain an environment that is supportive and nurturing. You do not have to be fancy, instead be intentional and purposeful in your planning, décor, room arrangement, management style and most of all, your delivery. Being consistent in your management, expectations, and routines allows your students to feel safe and ready to learn when in your learning space.

Data Dives and Action Plans in Primary

Understanding our students' strengths and needs by analyzing their data helps ease the angst of "what should I be teaching and what should they be learning?" Understanding your grade-level expectations and meeting the children where they are, ensures you are able to support them based on their individual needs.

Discussing data and creating an academic action plan with a child is so empowering. It helps both the educator and the child focus on their independent and emerging skills and provide them with strategies they will use to master the skill. It allows a child to align their early learning skills to their new academic expectations and gives them the ability to speak on their learning goals and gains.

When action plans are shared with a child's support systems, they feel empowered to support their child, the educator and school system alike, because they understand the areas of focus and what strategies they need to use to support their child's academic growth. This step is impactful to a child's academic foundation, career, and overall success.

Strengthening Foundational Skills

By supporting our primary scholar's foundational skillsets early on, allows them to successfully matriculate to the next grade level, understanding what they are working on, what they are successful at and what strategies they are using.

How do you support a child that has a strong basic academic foundation upon entering your class? By introducing age-appropriate academic rigor in our lessons, According to the Art of Education website, rigor is "work that challenges students' thinking in new and interesting ways. Promoting rigor in the classroom requires expectations and experiences that are academically, intellectually, and personally challenging."

When you know your students, their data, grade-level expectations and use it to guide your practice, you allow all levels of learners to flourish. Maria Montessori says *"The goal of Early Childhood Education should be to activate the child's own natural desire to learn."*

How will you activate your scholar's desire to learn? What about your desire to teach? What will be your action plan? How are you going to be intentional and purposeful, in and for your classroom?

As early childhood educators, we are the builders of our scholars' academic foundation, ensuring that they have the skills they need to be successful throughout their entire academic careers. The impact an early childhood educator has is tremendous, not only to each individual scholar, but to their support systems, the classroom, grade level, and the school as a whole. We have the ability to empower, inspire and encourage a child and their support system to be engaged, interested, and committed to their academic careers beginning in the early years.

As the saying goes, let's start by "working smarter, not harder!" and create action plans that support our early childhood educators in establishing academic readiness in our primary scholars. Let's focus on making early learning intentional and purposeful, because "when we learn together, we achieve together!" The Blooming Scholar

Rhea Watson
The Scholarship Doctor

Rhea M. Watson, The Scholarship Doctor, is a native of Las Vegas, NV and holds bachelor's and master's degrees from Morris Brown College and the University of Nevada, Las Vegas.

Rhea is the President and Founder of Scholarship Solutions, a premier Scholarship and College Consulting Firm. She works with students worldwide, ages six months to 90 years young. She is an international speaker, having presented to audiences in Egypt, England, Germany, Gabon, Jamaica, South Africa, and North America, teaching students of all ages how to have a debt-free college experience.

Personally, Rhea has earned over $300,000 in scholarships and has helped students enter the colleges of their dreams, winning more than $85 million in scholarships.

Rhea has a litany of accolades, including the United States Marines, Mentor of the Year and the US-Africa International Women's Day Award.

myscholarshipsolutions.com

Preparing for College in Kindergarten

By Rhea M. Watson

W hile putting together the final touches on a five-year-old's scholarship essay, there is a sigh of relief and a big smile matched with giggles and leaps complementing the satisfaction and accomplishment he exuded. In that moment, he believed he had put his best effort into the finished product and exclaimed, "I'm going to win!" and guess what, he did. Yes, a five-year-old. Yes, a college scholarship competition. Yes, this process can begin in kindergarten and before.

Amazingly and perhaps a bit unexpectedly, the scholarship and college preparation and application processes should begin at birth. In fact, I have worked with couples who engaged in this process during their family planning stage. Why? Because since one can begin earning scholarships at birth, there is no reason to wait until the senior year of high school.

To date, my youngest student to have applied for a college scholarship has been four months of age, the youngest scholarship winner has been age two, and incredibly, this same young student has won over twenty scholarships, grants, and contests. Above all, his college education is paid in full at the ripe age of five. How exciting!

Although this young scholar is a highly celebrated, quite calculated, and incredibly motivated little boy, he is not alone. I have been blessed to facilitate the efforts of dozens of elementary school children in the United States and abroad to apply for and win scholarships for college, and the beauty of starting early and applying often, is they will never experience the distresses of student loan debt.

Many times, I am asked how it is possible for a five-year-old to apply for scholarships. For instance, sometimes they are just learning their basic skills, right? Therefore, the idea of a young child completing the traditional steps of an application, essay, and submitting a stellar transcript and/or resume` may appear unfathomable. I am also often asked, "Where do you find scholarships for infants, toddlers, and young children?"

The nature of these questions suggests that people may have the belief that the scholarship process is unattainable or far too advanced/challenging for those who are very young. The concept of "Pre-K College Prep" is an area of concern for parents, educators, and community supporters. But my philosophy is to serve children at their maximum, whatever that is, and cultivate that potential with love, support, and mentorship. In doing so, a young student can and will excel at the scholarship and college preparation processes just like he or she will advance in any other areas that require the development of skills and abilities.

Actually, why don't we approach the scholarship and college processes like we do sports, music, or dance? Practically all athletic and artistic phenomena begin at birth. As a society, we have no problem cheering on our tiny tee ballplayers, beginning ballerinas, or early practicing pianists, to name a few. Parents proudly display team and individual photos of their young athletes. On college and professional signing days, they reminisce about how they "got to this point in life" by starting at their local community gym playing their particular sport as a young child.

In my extensive work related to scholarships and colleges, I must continually address two major myths: 1) Scholarship rewards and college preparation begin in high school; 2) It is the responsibility of Teachers and Counselors to assure students' scholarship and college successes. Unfortunately, these beliefs and behaviors have curated a culture of 1.7 trillion dollars in student loan debt in the United States. The cures to the student loan debt crises are to start scholarship and college preparation early, work on the processes often, and involve an entire team of family, coaches, educators, and mentors to assist students in winning at the scholarship and college game.

What are the next steps?

You may be wondering how to help your kindergarten student apply for college scholarships. Well, although the processes and procedures may be more simplified, the expectations and requirements are not extremely different from those of a high school or college student. Although I will provide a few examples of scholarships for which you and your young scholars can and should apply, here are some important foundational pieces that must be addressed:

- **Earn A and A Grades** - From day one, express the importance of strong grades/marks. We should encourage our children to earn A's and A's and compliment and celebrate their accomplishments in this regard. Setting this precedence is not a pressure point but rather an expectation that can be met and exceeded when proper planning and consistent academic support is in place. "A" grades are not the only variable in achieving scholarships, but strong grades must not be ignored.

- **The Power of Passion** - Passion projects are so important in relationship to scholarships. Young children see a need in the world and have incredible, brilliant, and brave ideas which can make eternal changes. They may talk about space, animals, their dolls, trucks, or other toys, cartoons, and whatever else resonates with them. Take the time to listen to their dreams and ideas so you can help them change a fantasy into a fantastic project. Be unafraid to help them cultivate creativity and character. Their dreams can become their passion projects which can set a pathway to scholarship winnings and debt-free college degree(s).

- **The Love of Leadership** - Leadership is a driving force in earning scholarships at any age. Children should be encouraged to work toward being elected or appointed to an office, whether it be in their first-grade classroom, girl or boy scouts, the church choir, or being the CEO of their own businesses. Involvement in extracurricular activities and having a leadership position will help students secure scholarships. This is the beginning of building their resume, to include leadership experiences, which will set them on a trajectory of success, security, and scholarship acquisition.

- **Think SMART, Take a STEM, and Feel the STEAM** - Science Math and Research Technology (SMART), Science Technology Engineering and Math (STEM), and Science, Technology, Engineering, Agriculture, and Math (STEAM) are important avenues to earning scholarships. In fact, those with SMART, STEM, and STEAM areas of study are 3.5 times more likely to receive a scholarship than students who have other college and professional aspirations. Therefore, start introducing students to SMART/STEM/STEAM education and extracurricular activities now. With organizations and programs like 4-H, Girls Who Code, Lego Clubs, NSBE Junior, and more, the opportunity to grow children's experiences, exposures, and education in these areas are endless. Find SMART/STEM/STEAM-focused groups and clubs for your children and get them involved in these majors so they can gain access to scholarship dollars early.

- **Standardized Test Preparation** - Although college entrance exams are introduced in the early part of middle school, elementary school children should be introduced to PSAT/ACT/SAT. When children have early and regular exposure and experiences with these exams, the less intimidating and ill-prepared they will be when it is time to score high on these tests. Specifically, students ages ten and older should be taking these exams and properly preparing for them through test prep courses and regular regimented study plans. When they are properly prepared and very well-practiced, they are able to secure the important test scores of 1350 PSAT, 1400 SAT, and 30 ACT. These scores contribute to large scholarship rewards and college acceptances. Additionally, when the proper planning, programming, and progressions are in place, students have secured the score they need and desire far in advance of the senior year, helping their last year of high school to be smooth, stressless, and strong.

- **Tackle Tough Subjects with Tutoring** - Please understand this: "Tutoring is for smart people, too!" The misconception is when a child is struggling, he or she needs help from a tutor. However, the best approach is to work with a tutor to gain and maintain strong A grades and to assist with subjects that may be challenging. This should be done for students far in advance of them needing help to survive a class or master a concept. It is important that every child has an academic dream team comprised of a Scholarship Coach, an Athletic or Artistic Coach, a Test Prep Coach, and an Academic Coach or Tutor. When this dream team is formulated and everyone is working in concert, the student is better positioned to soar academically and can easily achieve the goal of earning scholarships and attending college debt-free.

Things Every Kindergarten Student Should Do

The Kindergarten Checklist is a great way to stay on track with the path to scholarships and debt freedom. Incorporate these items in your everyday life and watch your scholarship garden bloom.

- Say out loud and read or write, "*I am going to college for free.*"

- Read daily.

- Join SMART/STEM/STEAM classes, clubs and other activities.

- Explore colleges and majors online and in person.

- Attend college fairs.

- Earn straight A's.

- Study for PSAT/ACT/SAT.

- Volunteer regularly.

- Start a college savings plan.

- Participate in sports, music, and other school and extracurricular activities and take a leadership role.

- Apply for as many scholarships as possible.

- Work with a tutor to tackle tough subjects.

Scholarships for Kindergarten Students

I am hopeful that after reading this information, you are empowered and ready to forge your student's scholarship path. Honestly, this chapter is packed with tools, tips, tactics, tricks, and techniques to help you and yours apply for and win scholarships. Now that you have the "how-to" for applying, here is a startup list of scholarships.

- Debbie's Dream Foundation Essay Contest - Grades K-12 (Up to $1000)

- Doodle 4 Google - Grades K - 12 (Up to $30,000)

- Eco Hero Award - Ages 8 - 16 (Up to $500)

- Stephen J. Brady - Ages 5 - 25 (Up to $5000)

- Wergle Flomp Humor Poetry Contest - Ages 0 - 100 (Up to $2000)

This is a small yet significant sample of attainable scholarships for which young children can apply. You have plenty of time, so don't delay - apply today!

What if you are beyond Kindergarten?

It is never too early and never too late to apply for scholarships. Although this chapter was created to enlighten and ignite opportunity and information to parents and educators, scholarships are available to anyone and everyone. However, if you or your student are pursuing any form of higher education, please apply for scholarships to help underscore and supplement your educational expenses, without having to disrupt household budgets or savings. If you have a middle school, high school, or college student, use these same principles and apply for scholarships. If you are a current college or graduate student, apply for scholarships. Whatever stage you are in, it is the perfect time to secure debt freedom. In fact, the majority of my clients start their scholarship journey in high school and have humongous successes with their scholarship ambitions. I am overly confident that you can and will do the same. I believe in you. You got this! Now, let's go to college debt FREE!

Roberta Coleman
Special Education Expert

Called to be a life-changer for today's generation, Roberta Coleman is a vibrant, energetic, no-nonsense educator! She has an undeniable passion for empowering others, especially youth, to maximize their God-given potential. She uses her powerful gift to teach both within and beyond the four walls of the classroom.

Born in Liberia, West Africa, Roberta and her family relocated to the United States in 1981. She attended North Carolina Agricultural and Technical State University and graduated with a Bachelor of Science degree in Psychology. She continued to matriculate to Walden University, where she earned a Master's in Elementary Reading and Literacy and became an honor graduate. Along with her educational accomplishments, Mrs. Coleman is the recipient of numerous awards and distinctions.

With over 23 years of experience in the field of education, Mrs. Coleman has served in many capacities. Currently, she is a special education teacher and founder of Intentional Services for Students, a consulting program supporting parents of a students with special needs. She is devoted to and intentional about every child's individual learning and life success. She offers fresh, insightful truths that encourage all individuals, especially educators and young people, to make the best use of their God-given potential in their personal and professional lives.

www.iss4you.com

Better Educational Habits

By Roberta Bombo Coleman

I n 1998, I walked into a school seeking a position as a teacher assistant. Prior to that, I worked at a daycare as a Pre-K-3 teacher. When I walked into the interview, I was nervous because I did not have a teaching degree. I had a degree in psychology. What was supposed to be a 30-minute interview turned out to be a two-hour interview.

The administrator who interviewed me asked if I was willing to take a teaching position instead of the assistant position. He said, "We have a group of students that need you and what you have to offer." I asked about the students and the class I would be teaching, and he hesitated for a while. Finally, he said, "Well, Ms. Bombo, you are going to teach the BEH class." I sat there puzzled, trying to figure out exactly what he meant by BEH.

He told me that BEH meant that they are behaviorally and emotionally handicapped. He explained they couldn't seem to keep teachers in that class and the students were a handful. I told him I would accept the position until they could find a teacher that was certified to teach these students since I knew nothing about special education.

It was two days before the start of the school year. I felt unprepared and somewhat afraid of what was ahead. I read the students' files. The files gave me what I needed to know to begin the school year. It contained a summary of all evaluation results, a record of each student's specific category of disability or, in the case of reevaluation, whether the student continues to have such a disability. Each child's present levels of performance and educational needs that result from the disability were all there written in black and white.

Some of the students needed related services to help them meet the measurable annual goals in the IEP and to participate, as appropriate, in the general curriculum. All the students were three or more years behind their peers. Many of them had traumatic experiences and lived in group homes or community homes. I was thinking to myself, "Roberta, what have you gotten yourself into?" I took a deep breath and began to plan.

I was not going to be another warm body in the classroom. I wanted *all* of these students to learn and grow, but I had to give special attention to them because they were the most vulnerable and fragile children who may have wished to be in school and learning but weren't given opportunities to do so. Having come to the U.S. from a third-world country, I understood the value of education not only because it can change lives positively, but also because it is a stimulus for community development, peace, security, and our hope for the future. To do that, I had to change the narrative. I needed a strong message that clearly identified what we were trying to achieve and why a narrative change was necessary.

The language and the words we use can have a profound impact on our success and well-being. I walked into the office and asked the administrator if I could change the name of my class from "behavioral and emotional handicapped" class to a sign that read Better Educational Habits class. Those words became "our story."

I knew changing the words would chang the meaning of what was going to happen in our classroom. It would change my students' internal representations and how they saw themselves and things. It was going to shift their feelings about school and help them be more empowered, less stressed and provide a sense of calmness. If we as educators want to change the narrative and help students develop better educational habits, we must be willing to do the following.

Begin by creating a positive learning environment. It has often been said that children don't care about what you know until they know you care. Many studies have shown that there is a direct relationship between the kind of learning environment teachers create in their classrooms and student achievement. Our classrooms must address our students' needs. Students have physical needs, but they also have psychological needs for security and order, love and belonging, personal power and competence and freedom.

When we as educators intentionally address these needs in the classroom, students are happier to be there, behavior incidents occur far less frequently, and student engagement and learning increases. If we want them to learn, that learning must address their needs. Ignoring needs creates an environment where our students become stagnant and develop fixed mindsets.

Don't just be there, be present. Make every day an adventure filled with learning for students and yourself. Don't show up because it's a job. Show up for your students. Advocate for and support them. If you want to engage your students, you must do more than just show up. You must allow them to feel your presence not just with your body, but with your mind. Seize every moment to not only connect but teach.

Teachable moments come up all the time in our classrooms. As educators, we must pay close attention and be ready for them. We must be willing to engage with student questions and have open and honest dialogues. Taking the time to explain the "why" behind the answer to a student's question is often one of the best ways to create a teachable moment. You can also create teachable moments by asking students to talk about their favorite sports, role model, or what's happening in the world.

For this generation, the coronavirus pandemic and the social injustices will be the markers of everything that was before and now everything is different, so it is important to stay physically, mentally, and emotionally connected with them and their families and community. I remember when I first started teaching. I had all boys in my class. I grew up with mostly sisters, so I knew little or nothing about what boys were into. I asked questions about what they liked.

I found out that they were into wrestling, football, basketball, and rap. Every Monday night, I would stay up watching wrestling to send them a message that I care about their interests. Even Though I barely understood football, I watched the games. I would come in asking them questions about the game, and we switched roles where the teacher became their pupil. The students loved it. This got them talking to me about their fears and struggles. I was able to use sports as a cross-reference in class and something they could relate to. If we want them to do better, we have to be better.

In order to change what the students are doing, we have to change what we are doing. When I got into that classroom and had no clue about special education, I went to my alma mater North Carolina Agricultural and Technical University and enrolled in their certification program. I was not going to do these students a disservice.

We can't just fake it until we make it. Our students have to see us as lifelong learners. They saw me reading books. I would purposely make a mistake in class and give them an opportunity to catch and correct my mistakes. I remember being told that it is not the special education teacher's responsibility to know the core. That angered me because it is very important for all teachers to learn and understand what they are teaching and the standards they are teaching. We must understand the content and contextualize it, so that it becomes relevant to our students, especially in special ed.

If we lack the knowledge of a curriculum, we won't be able to know whether students are developing a rooted foundation to continue learning at the next level. If we don't know the standards or outcomes that students are expected to know for each course or grade level, then it will be difficult to know what to teach. Knowing what to teach at each grade level means knowing where we must focus our efforts to strengthen students' understanding. We must be purposeful in our planning. These four questions should guide our planning:

1. What can the student do?

2. What can't the student do?

3. How does the student's work compare with that of others?

4. How can I help the student do better?

It is extremely important to give students effective feedback. Feedback encourages student growth. Too many young people do not see themselves as being academically capable in school. If we want to develop better educational habits in the classroom, we must listen to their stories to gauge why learning has been a struggle, then use their experience as a guide to be a better teacher for them.

I absolutely love watching students grow into confident learners, and I love watching them learn how to support one another. No other role in a school, positions you to witness this beautiful human transformation. Authentic, purposeful learning occurs when students are given the opportunity to grasp and apply their learning through revision and application. Students need to reflect on their proficiency on different levels and develop a game plan.

What we assess and how we assess sends a powerful message to our students about what we value. This can have a powerful impact on learning. Using our students' work samples is an effective way to help guide their peer-to-peer and teacher/student feedback. Unless we ask the right questions, feedback won't be very useful.

In order to change how they are performing, we have to change how we address the gaps in our students' learning. This means making time to reteach/address misconceptions before moving forward. We should also use exemplars to show students how to take the weakest parts of their work to the next level! We should also create enrichment opportunities to encourage growth in students even after they have mastered the standards, such as learning progression scales in various curriculum.

Learning progression is the sequencing of teaching and learning expectations across multiple developmental stages, ages, or grade levels. They are categorized and organized by content areas, such as mathematics or writing, and they map out a specific sequence of knowledge and skills that students are expected to learn as they progress through each grade level. The progression will help the teacher and the student understand where the student currently is on the progression. It helps teachers determine which steps are needed next for that student to continue working towards mastery of the grade-level standards.

With this information, the teacher can deconstruct the standards into specific learning targets, clearly communicate the learning targets into student-friendly terms with students and encourage students to set goals for themselves as they are learning to develop self-efficacy. Remember the purpose of good feedback is to improve student learning.

Over the past 23 years, I have worked with students both in the public and private sectors. Nothing is more fulfilling like parents writing to thank me for helping their child succeed. I often encounter parents who are frustrated and feel overwhelmed. They don't understand how certain skills are taught now because that's not how they learned these skills when they were in school.

I remember one student in particular whose parents asked me to work with a couple of years ago. Alex was a smart kid who lacked confidence with the belief that he was not as smart as the other kids in his class or grade. Through working with the young man and his parents using the growth mindset approach, Alex was accepted into the gifted program at his school. I have so many stories that I could share. Using these principles will help instill better educational habits in all students.

Erin Bennett
An Informed Parent

Erin Bennett is a writer and working mom from North Carolina. She attended East Carolina as a Teaching Fellow but says that as a "gifted child" she was quite a snob about her abilities so she left. She leads a successful career in finance. Notoriously bad at math, she's been in banking for nearly two decades, where, in addition to providing financial solutions, she enjoys dissecting emails from colleagues and judging their use of commas. She and her husband James were high school sweethearts. In addition to raising chickens and bees, they share two sons, happily shuttling them to baseball games and guitar practice. Raising her children has shown her that while labels and classifications are helpful to understanding people, they have no bearing on how successful a child will be. She is grateful her sons will know the value of hard work.

Instagram: @ern_chicka_ern.

Remote Learning

By Erin Bennett

There continues to be angst around the impact of the pandemic, especially on schools. Here we are after almost two years of masking and social distancing, and what we thought would be our "post-pandemic" life, is not quite that at all. My husband, our 16-year-old, and I are fully vaccinated as we await approval for my ten-year-old to be. They are back in school and doing much better, which confirms my choice to keep them at home last year. In reflection of where we were then, here's my story.

There are many voices urging the return to in-person learning, but you won't find mine among them. That's not to say remote learning has been easy, or that my choice to keep my child home even as his school has slowly re-opened has come without sacrifice. My husband and I both work, I manage a team, and all of this requires a balance so fragile that a late phone call or a missing assignment can throw the entire system out of whack. But the impact that remote learning has had on my ten-year-old son Henry this year makes our choice to keep him home a no-brainer.

In the beginning, it was easy. Everyone was staying home. While other parents ran around like their hair was on fire complaining about how they should arrange childcare or struggling to navigate the fifteen websites for which their child had logins, Henry and I tucked in. Come August,

COVID-19 rates in our county were higher than they'd been in March, but schools re-opened anyway (albeit on an A Day/B Day rotation). Parents said, "Thank goodness! I couldn't keep these kids home one more minute!" But I demurred, insisting that we were waiting for rates to go down.

Sometime before winter break, the elementary schools in our district went to in-person instruction four days a week, but again I demurred. "We are caretakers for my husband's grandmother, and we can't risk the exposure," I told the school (knowing full well she'd been ordering groceries online on her own since April).

But now? Vaccinations are rising, infection rates are lowering, and I am running out of excuses. There will come a day where my flexibly scheduled workdays will have worn out their welcome with my boss, where the special education teacher at Henry's school will no longer offer Zoom sessions, and we will no longer be able to use COVID-19 as an excuse. Eventually, Henry will have to return to school.

Isn't he excited about this? Doesn't he miss his friends? Oh, he sure does. He misses them terribly. And so, imagine how much he must carry in his tiny little heart to miss his friends so badly and yet still be so adamant that he does not want to go back.

In March 2020, just as COVID-19 was really kicking off, I was nearing what I hoped was the end of a years-long battle to put my finger on what was going on with Henry. He was nearing the end of his third-grade year and I felt that the time for us to make adjustments, try interventions, or otherwise keep him from falling through the cracks was running out.

After countless interventions and parent-teacher conferences and Summer reading programs, I was walking out of a psychologist's office—a private one I'd paid for out of pocket—with a diagnosis: Attention Deficit Hyperactivity Disorder (ADHD) and Learning Disability-Reading Comprehension and Writing. My baby was dyslexic.

My hope for the diagnosis was that it would help me understand more of what Henry needed. But I also hoped it would spur some action from his school. Perhaps if I gave them this clue, this key to my child, the teachers and administrators would suddenly unveil all these solutions and support he had needed for so long that we had been unable to articulate properly. We could stop talking about levels and interventions and all the ways his performance was being artificially propped up in order to meet some requirements or ensure some funding. We could now get to the heart of what was going on.

I sent the paperwork containing the psychologist's assessment to all the appropriate people and waited for appointments and conferences to be scheduled. In the meantime, Henry and I got to work making up for lost time. Every morning we would get up together and go over all the assignments listed in Google Classroom. I would read them out loud as he followed along, then have him make a checklist of what his work was so he could check it off as he went.

I let him choose which subject he would start with, but he likes routine and so would typically choose Science/Social Studies, then English Language Arts, then Math. If he was stuck on something, we'd move to something else and come back. If he was having trouble staying focused, he would go walk the dog or have a snack. And I was right by his side, making sure that he clearly understood the task. Often, I would re-teach the lesson for him once he'd watched the instructional video.

For the first time in Henry's life, he was making A's and B's. But more than that, he was enjoying the process of learning. I know that for other parents whose children get called up to the stage every quarterly awards ceremony to accept their honor roll certificates, these conversations about children falling behind as a result of remote learning are very compelling.

But for us, school was never about which prestigious university Henry would be accepted into. We did not look for a certain grade or a certain award. We measured success in other ways. Is his head down on his desk or is he sitting up and working? Is he asking good questions? How much prompting did he require for a written response? Little by little, his confidence grew and his desire to engage, to take chances even, increased.

When he got back his first school project with a gold star and a 96 on it, we had to leave it on the refrigerator for a month. I was proud of him, but more than that, he was proud of himself. This is what I had been fighting for.

So it was a struggle when, at our first IEP (Individualized Education Plan) meeting of the year, just as fourth grade started, I was encouraged to take a more hands-off approach. "We need to be able to see what he does on his own," they said, "so that we can properly assess him." Wasn't that the basis of the psychologist's report?

I reminded them of the parent-teacher conferences we'd been having every year going back to kindergarten. I mentioned how his first-grade teacher had gotten cancer a few months into the school year and his class had a series of substitute teachers every day from October to June. I brought up how I'd asked if he could be failed, held back, etc. that year, because he was already so far behind and had gotten no response.

I referred to the seemingly endless levels of interventions, how there's always another level, how there never seems to be a point where we say, "You know what, this kid is just not getting it; let's think of something else." I had already burned through four years of elementary school waiting on an answer and I wasn't willing to let another one go by while they tried to figure out what to do. The clock was ticking. So, we stayed home. I stayed hands-on. Henry stayed successful.

We had conversations about going back to school in the Fall when fifth grade begins. I told Henry it will be good to be around his friends again. I told him he has made so much progress and he will do well. But he looked back at me and said he was not so sure. "I will have to rush around all day from thing to thing and I won't be able to ever finish," he said. "I won't be able to rewind the video if I don't understand something, or have them read it to me, or take a break when I get frustrated," he said. I asked him what I can do to help with that, but the truth is there's so much that could be done and it's way too much to fall onto his little shoulders. But there are some important steps that I think can be considered now that we are on the other side of the pandemic.

More teachers. It's a tale as old as time, I know, but it's an obvious need. Teachers have borne the brunt of the pandemic creating remote learning on the fly while maintaining in-person teaching. They deserve to have less on their plate so they can focus more on their craft. And for children like my son who thrive in a more personalized setting, more teachers would mean he is much more likely to get the attention he needs to succeed.

More free time during the instructional day. A huge challenge for Henry in the classroom is only having a small amount of time for a task before being transitioned to the next activity. Without individual attention, he struggles to conceptualize what is expected of him, and by the time he finally understands the work, time is up and he's being moved to the next thing.

I understand that this is likely a result of all that teachers are expected to cover in a day. But so much of our learning time at home is spent having a conversation about the lesson that was just taught, him asking questions, him taking a break because he is getting frustrated — these are things that there isn't time for when you are moving 30 children through 7 subjects all before the bell rings at 2:30.

A reevaluation of expectations for self-management I think I was in high school before I understood what a rubric was, but my 9-year-old has a rubric assigned with every class project. Is he supposed to be able to read that and understand all the criteria? Is it appropriate to expect an elementary school student to be able to navigate Google Classroom on their own, keeping up with passwords for ancillary sites and ensuring all assignments listed in the teacher's paragraph-form lesson plan were completed? I'm asking as a 37-year-old woman who regularly locks herself out of her Netflix account.

75

Moving away from grade-level expectations. My son does not read at grade level, and he likely never will. As someone who will never meet the BMI standard my doctor wants me at, I sympathize. Perhaps instead of setting one standard that all children, regardless of background, ability, starting point, etc., should meet, why aren't we instead measuring progress? What a terrible thing to have a child work so hard, and teacher interventions work so well, only to have to tell that child that they will be attending the summer reading program yet again despite their effort. How long would you try if that were the answer? I've had to remind Henry several times that grades don't matter. Let's think of a new way he can measure himself without worrying about how he stacks up to everyone else.

Teachers should become advisors. How long is my child supposed to fail before someone brings it to my attention? What if I were less educated, less curious, less aware, unable to source help privately and independent of the school system? Listen, they simply handed me this child and wheeled me out of the hospital—there are no degrees or certifications for this. I need help.

I depend on my son's teachers, administrators, and faculty to be in my village and give me expert advice. You can ask me if I'm okay with going to the next level of intervention, but I don't have a clue what that means. You can ask me if I'd like to have this type of EC pull-out or that, but I'll just nod and smile. Oh, how I wish someone had come to me sooner and said, "We think Henry has dyslexia, you may want to test him" or "Henry is not performing up to grade level and we've been doing interventions all year, we need to talk about whether it's appropriate to move him on."

But instead, I get recommendations to read to him more at home or set up a behavior chart or simply *medicate*. And while all those things may be tools that help, they won't work on their own. While staff bites their tongue and wrings their hands to avoid offending litigious parents, my child continues to move from grade to grade without either of us knowing what to do.

Consider remote instruction as a part of regular school. Think of all the possibilities for accommodating several unique learning styles in a classroom if the technology we've come to rely on through the pandemic could be leveraged long-term. Better yet, what if children were grouped by learning style so that those who benefit from more one-on-one instruction that remote learning has provided could continue to be successful? This could be done while those high-achieving children who have struggled at home could remain in the traditional class setting. Or, rather than having all students in the class do independent work while the teacher does small group work at his or her table, why not leverage remote instruction for small group so that the students are always engaged?

To paraphrase Jon Snow, *Autumn is coming.* When August rolls back around and fifth grade is upon us, I won't have any more reasons to keep Henry at home. Even if remote learning is an option provided by the school, continuing on is not sustainable for me and other working parents whose bosses are still not ready to accept full-time remote work as an option. And honestly, I need to go back.

As much as I have enjoyed using this time to get Henry caught up, to help him see how fun learning can be, the fact is teaching children and working full-time cannot be done at the same time long-term. I know teachers bristle when parents make jokes about needing schools to open so they can get rid of these kids. We know you aren't babysitters: you're highly skilled professionals, key members of the village that we rely on to help us get these kids to adulthood. Because if I've learned anything this past year, it's that I can't do it by myself.

I'll always be a believer in community schools. But I urge parents, as well as teachers, to stop viewing the end of this school year as the finish line: "I can't wait until next school year when things can just get back to normal." There will still be many unknowns. Will children be able to transition back into the classroom? Will they remember how to be around their peers, how to manage themselves in a classroom, how to do work at a desk rather than the kitchen table? How much learning loss will there be?

Will we be able to make up any losses using the typical techniques that I'm sure teachers use to address Summer regression? Or do we need to reconsider standards of measurement? And what about the children like Henry who flourished during remote learning? Will they be allowed to continue learning in a way that best suits them, or will they be forced to go back to the old patterns that caused so much discouragement before?

In other words, will the past year that we spent during the pandemic be a blip, a mistake, something to quickly move on from and forget? Should we just "get back to normal?" Or does a return to school present an opportunity for us to reconsider what exactly that normal should be? Has "normal" been working? For Henry, the answer is a resounding: No!

As a principal friend of mine recently put it, "The bottom line is, if we have found a way that kids learn the best, that's the way they should be taught." Instead of rushing back to what we know, what if we used this time to figure out how to keep the ways our kids learn best and get rid of all the things that weren't serving us before?

As fourth grade draws to a close for Henry, I will resist the urge to let him run feral all Summer so that I can focus on work. This year has been a hard one and we are all tired, but we can't take our feet off the gas just yet, mamas. As much as we need these teachers (Please come get our kids!), these teachers need us, too. It's going to take every week of this coming Summer to get Henry to remember how to go to bed at 8:30 p.m., how to get up before 10 a.m., what is breakfast, what are pants, is that the Sun? If you thought Summer Learning Loss was bad, we now have Rona Learning Loss to deal with on top of it.

Our kids have been through a lot, and they deserve a thoughtful transition back into the classrooms that we used to take for granted. In many ways, this feels like that one last Summer before we sent them off to kindergarten. We spent time teaching them how to tie their shoes. We made sure they could say their teacher's name, we made sure they got a good night's sleep.

When the day came to drop them off, there were some parents who barely slowed the car down while they rolled the kid out onto the sidewalk; while others lingered by the door just a little too long, wanting to make sure their baby was okay. Excitement and grief, relief and anxiety, holding our breath until they step off the bus after that first day. Another level achieved. A new normal.

Monica D. Thompson
Speech Pathologist

Monica D. Thompson is a native of High Point, NC. She earned a Bachelor of Science degree in Family and Consumer Sciences and a Master of Education Degree in Communication Sciences and Disorders from North Carolina Central University. Monica is a Speech Language Pathologist and has been in the field working with children and adults with communication disorders for over 12 years. She has a passion for youth and young adults with disabilities and would like to one day develop educational policies that will support and allow educators to effectively and efficiently assess/evaluate students. She is currently a doctoral student in the Educational Leadership and Management Program at Drexel University. In her spare time, Monica enjoys traveling, reading, walking, watching movies, spending time with family and friends, singing, and writing children's songs.

speechmonicathompson@gmail.com

I Look Different on Paper

By Monica D. Thompson

As a Speech Language Pathologist working in public schools, I frequently have witnessed students with inappropriate educational placements. There is a glitch in the evaluation process that has caused an increase in the over-and-under identification of students with disabilities. These recurring issues include students who need special services and do not receive them, students receiving services that do not truly need them, and/or incorrect educational placement and classification of students.

After more than 12 years as an educator, working in northern and southern states as well as urban and rural schools, I realize this has become a perpetual problem. Anyway, we look at it; something is wrong when this is happening all over the country. How do we stop an insufficient cycle? How do we improve the system and the way we do things? The ever-increasing focus of my work is to provide solutions that will bring about change and resolve.

In most cases, students are judged by what people read about them before anyone ever lays eyes on them. First impressions are everything. Educators read information that has been collected by reputable sources such as medical reports, grades, attendance, test results, behavior and discipline issues, trauma, psychological evaluations, etc.

Even we as adults get judged by our resume, job performance, driving record, and social-emotional well-being. Often it does not tell the whole story and what is written is not always true. Information that is reported is based on what someone else perceives or interprets about us or, in some cases, what we think about ourselves. Students don't get to tell their story or their truth. Instead, professionals decide what is best for them. Many of them look different on paper than they do when interacting with educators and classmates.

Assessments are used as tools to determine a child's strengths and weaknesses or to further investigate academic concerns. In public schools, the criteria to qualify a student for related services (Occupational, Physical, and Speech Therapy) must meet a specific score. Anything below this number qualifies a student for special education services. Anything above this number indicates that the child does not meet the criteria for special education services and insinuates that there is no evidence that anything is interfering with his/her ability to access the academic curriculum.

What if this number does not reflect the difficulties the student is actually having? Why are we limited to this number? The number is valuable, but it is also a ballpark. For example, I worked with a six-year-old male student who scored an 83 on an articulation assessment. This score indicates that he was non-eligible for services, but he was still demonstrating sound errors that should have been mastered between four and five years old.

Should we select him for speech services or allow him to continue with these articulation difficulties? On paper, we would say "no," but when observing this student in the classroom, gathering input from his teacher, and examining interactions with his peers, the answer should be "yes." His articulation difficulties were affecting his ability to read, specifically with learning and processing sounds.

In this case, on paper, this child did not qualify, but in reality, he really needed the services. The prognosis was good and the student only required services on a short-term basis because he was motivated to meet goals and retain and learn information quickly. Short-term actions lead to long-lasting outcomes. We must consider all the factors when making a decision about whether or not a student should qualify for services, as we cannot always rely on a number to base our decision.

I received a speech referral for another student in kindergarten with academic and behavior concerns, who had a history of neglect and abuse from his biological parents. When I began working with this child, he had recently been placed in foster care and his biological parents had relinquished their parental rights due to substance abuse. His case history provided evidence that this child was suffering from trauma; dealing with varied emotions and feelings affected his ability to access the academic curriculum.

At the eligibility determination meeting, it was reported that this student was classified as having Autism Spectrum Disorder. I was completely surprised by this decision. Speech/Language test results, interactions with the student, observations, and teacher input did not reflect this classification. Was this a mistake? Did they gather the necessary data and case history to support this diagnosis? Do they know his particular circumstances? Did something happen in the evaluation? I was thinking surely the information got mixed up, but this was the final verdict. This child was going to be categorized as Autistic.

Once they placed him in the autistic support classroom with peers his age, everything went downhill. His behavior became worse. He began mocking his classmate's repetitive body movements and behaviors, making jokes, and displaying other inappropriate mannerisms. Participation decreased and he refused to work in small groups. He only wanted to receive one-on-one support. This child was not acting like his usual self. In my opinion, these behaviors were a cry for help. Acting out to gain attention, so someone could identify what was really going on with him. It was clearly obvious that this new educational placement was not improving the situation.

Everything about this situation disturbed me, so I challenged the reliability and validity of this evaluation and placement. I changed this decision by suggesting that this child be re-evaluated in order to determine the most appropriate placement. After consulting with his teacher and advocating on his behalf to the Special Education Liaison, a consent for re-evaluation was developed.

I was on the edge of my seat until the results were complete. The test data concluded that he, indeed, did not fit the category of AU (autism) but would be classified as having an emotional disability. This was not a total resolve to the issue, but a start in the right direction toward increasing his academic growth and success.

Possible solutions to the problem

Prior to conducting assessments, educators will determine if an evaluation is necessary by utilizing the school's intervention program and designated team members. This program is designed to identify students who are lacking the necessary skills required to fully access the educational curriculum, are at risk of failure, and/or retention. Information obtained in this process would better guide the decision-making progress and fully determine if testing is needed to further investigate academic or behavioral concerns. Interventions should be developed to address areas of concern and implemented on a consistent basis to properly measure growth or progress. Data collection and progress monitoring are the key components that will guide the decision-making process. The main purpose of conducting interventions is to determine if the child can make progress with extra one-on-one help addressing areas of concern and to rule out all other factors that could possibly contribute to a decline in academic performance, including lack of exposure, suspected disability, learning difference, and/or other external factors.

Once the intervention plan has been developed, progress monitoring should be conducted on the recommended timeline that the intervention team has agreed upon. The intervention team should meet regularly to discuss the child's response to interventions, rate progress or regression, and re-adjust the plan if necessary. Progress is being made. A referral for an evaluation should be the last resort. A substantial amount of evidence is required to justify the need for further testing. Educators can be so quick to refer without saying, "Have I really done all that I can do?" A referral for a special education evaluation is a short-term approach, but not a resolution to the real issue. As educators, our responsibility is to identify and distinguish learning differences, lack of exposure, and the inability to learn and retain information in a general education setting.

Our responsibility is to collect and gather evidence that would support a Comprehensive Evaluation. The evaluation process can be compared to building a house. If the foundation is not solid, the entire house will fall apart. We need the necessary tools and materials to keep the foundation steady and well supported above ground, so that students can thrive and succeed academically. The tools that we need to gather include the following.

- medical information,

- home life

- social/emotional history

- educational experiences before the elementary setting

- academic performance, performance-based test

- classroom observations

- behavior (in and outside of the classroom)

- attendance, grades, sample work highlighting the academic concerns, data collected using interventions

- teacher/parent input

If any of this information is not included, we, as educators, have failed. These tools and materials are mandatory, not optional. We cannot include some; we need all of them.

Educators should not include surface-level information but must dig deep to obtain details in order to interpret results and make accurate decisions so that the person that we see at school matches the person that we write on paper.

Work together, not separate

Not only are comprehensive evaluations and results vital to determine the best educational placement, but collaboration with other educators is just as important. Often everyone is working individually and not as a team. This is not a one-man show, and there is no "I" in team. Without strategic and intentional collaboration, how can we ensure what is best for the student overall?

I have attended a dozen evaluation result meetings that were unorganized, not well thought out, and no one was aware of each person's roles and responsibilities. This results in incomplete and unprofessional meetings with no known real solution or plan to effectively provide services that would benefit or support the child academically. There needs to be a meeting before the meeting. A discussion prior to the meeting will allow educators to compare sources, express concerns or ideas, and make sure that necessary information has been collected.

When educators collaborate, it is obvious, and parents will notice whether or not everyone is on the same page. Collaboration takes time and effort—focused time that we seldom have, and effort to manage everyone's different point-of-view, so we can formulate a decision together. The team should work collectively to develop a plan, while individually managing roles and responsibilities required for the team.

Collaboration produces a sense of confidence and trust for the parent when they know that everyone is working together with one goal in mind, to help their child. Educators and parents need to work collaboratively to determine what is best for the child. Parents know their child more than anyone, but I also think it is good to consider a student's needs and wants from their own perspective. Periodically I will ask my students ``Is there anything that you would like to work on?" And to my surprise, I sometimes get a response.

One of my students responded, "Yes! Ms. Thompson, I would like to work on the "Q" sound. Not only was this student motivated to do his best, but he was fully aware of his own strengths and weaknesses, which in my opinion, is always beneficial information for evaluation but also progress monitoring.

Most would consider this to be a rarity, but have we considered what the child is thinking? Their thoughts and feelings are essential when making decisions regarding academic progress and interventions. We often don't think to include their perspective because they are children, and we think adults are the only ones capable of making informed decisions about them.

Would getting the student's perspective help us to come to a more informed decision regarding disability classification? How can we change the assessment and evaluation process to make it more holistic and comprehensive? Collaboration generates positive outcomes. It eliminates necessary errors or mistakes, to decrease the over and under-identification of students with special needs. In most cases, the person on paper is most reflected by the person who knows himself the most, the child.

Maxed out caseloads, excessive amounts of documentation, progress monitoring, individual education plan (IEP) meetings, strict 60–90-day deadlines, and Winter/Spring headcount interfere with a person's ability to do their best. In most cases, educators don't have the time in their workday to conduct or write a thorough assessment and/or evaluation, even if they have the desire or means to do so.

Educators are pressured to the point where they are more concerned about meeting restrictive deadlines than focusing on producing quality paperwork. They are in the rat race to have as many IEPs compliant as possible. We are humans, not machines or miracle workers. Thorough, detailed, and precise documentation takes time to develop. Evaluators need time to analyze and synthesize information to make decisions that will benefit the needs of students, while considering all key factors and indicators.

People are inclined to make mistakes when they are rushed and overwhelmed. This results in important pieces of information getting overlooked as well as outdated, incorrect, and incomplete paperwork. I have witnessed documentation with duplicated IEP goals, present levels, and service delivery times. Often, no changes or updates were made at all.

When the document does not indicate any progress, but just mere continuation, it is as if the child is at a standstill, not moving up or down. Why go through all these extreme measures, just to "look" compliant? Who really suffers in the end? The student. Students that need to be dismissed from services are continued on an outdated plan. There are those who have met goals but this is not recorded, as there are no new plans.

An extension of compliance deadlines would be a significant help. Some educators have caseloads ranging from 35-90 children. I have experienced caseloads from a range of those numbers as well. For example, if a school receives 11-14 referrals at one time, educators are responsible for completing that paperwork usually within a 60-day window of gaining parental consent.

How in the world would they complete that in that restrictive amount of time? Completely impossible! I am not suggesting the solution is to prolong the evaluation process without reasonable cause but allow extra time to produce a valuable product without the limitations. This timeline should be flexible. As long as the IEP team communicates with parents and provides intervention support during the evaluation process educators can ensure the student receives the adequate support needed.

Another limitation in this process is the lack of assessment tools due to funding. Some districts can't afford to keep up with the latest assessments. They simply use the same few tests over and over, even when the assessment, in most cases, is not appropriate. I have often inquired about other assessments and have been told there was only one copy which was being used in a rotation amongst clinicians across the county. How can I evaluate with the necessary tools? The wait prolongs the process. When children receive scores that are borderline for qualifying and not meeting the criteria, educators have a difficult time getting additional resources for further testing due to limited resources.

In a perfect "IEP world," the solution is smaller caseloads, more time, more staff, and increased funding. This would ensure that documentation reflects an evaluation process that has produced quality and not quantity results. These quality results should reflect one child and that child should look the same in person as s/he does on paper. What's on paper and what happens with the child I work with in person should be consistent. They are not two different things, but one in the same. We need to put an end to confusing the two so educators and other support providers are able to meet students' needs. I hope that in the future, we can abort this cycle and create an evaluation process that ensures that e child succeeds.

Dr. E'Toyare Williams
Campus Special Education Director

Dr. E'Toyare "Torie" Williams was born and raised in Kansas City, Missouri and graduated from Paseo Academy High School. After receiving her Bachelors of Science in Psychology from the University of Central Missouri in Warrensburg, she took her education further by completing her Masters of Art in Teaching (MAT) with an emphasis in Special Education from National- Louis University in Chicago. In addition to her MAT, Dr. Williams earned her Master of Business Administration (MBA). Dr. Williams received her Doctorate of Education from Chicago State University in December of 2019. At Thornridge High School, where she worked for 12 years, Dr. Williams was the Director of Student Activities. "Be VicTORIEus with Dr. Torie Williams," is an educational program that encourages the professional development of the individual and provides actionable guidance to help address ACEs by offering a fresh perspective and an independent point of view while guiding a process that fosters the growth and educational development of the individual.

Instagram: @dr.vicTORIEus

ACEs: What Happens During Childhood

By Dr. E'Toyare Williams

E very day, adolescents must transform into respectable students when attending school to meet their academic needs, whether it is face-to-face interaction or virtual. Outside of school, students are experiencing life as they see it through the COVID-19 lens. Depending on the situation, students go home and have to endure different types of abuse, neglect, and household challenges, that have an impact on them as students. They awaken the next day, having to transform into students again, carrying the burdens they have been experiencing growing up as adolescents. This cycle is repeated until they are old enough to move out of the household. In most cases, students carry those household dysfunctions with them daily.

When students were able to attend school before the COVID-19 pandemic, many entered their classrooms weighed down by worries and challenges outside of their control. These situations often led to poor attendance and discipline issues, including dropping out of school, or ended up in a juvenile detention center. These challenges are called Adverse Childhood Experiences (ACES). ACES can present critical problems for students. They can lead to health conditions such as stress and depression, and these are two of the many reasons why students are absent or have disciplinary issues.

According to the Center for Disease Control (CDC), these experiences are an important health issue. understanding the impetus of students' negative behaviors might be difficult, but it could help to determine what triggers these behaviors and how to implement interventions that might discourage these behaviors.

Since 1998, evidence has demonstrated the prevalence of different types of adverse or potentially traumatizing experiences, meaning ACES, which can happen during childhood. In response, many studies have demonstrated the benefits of trauma-informed practices in mental health. Some students who endured ACES suffer lasting effects that can impact their health. To address some of the attendance issues and school discipline in high school, school district administrators should address the needs of the students who have faced ACES.

At my former high school, I remember watching a student run to class late. I watched the teacher close the door in her face because she was tardy. What the teacher didn't realize until after talking to the student, is that she had to take public transportation to get to the school because no one was at home with her. Her grandmother was in the hospital, recovering from cancer. She was living with her grandmother temporarily because her mother was incarcerated. I did not know at the time, but after completing research, she had ACEs. The experiences with the majority of the students were all too familiar to me. I have heard several stories from my students. From physical, sexual, and verbal abuse from family members to having incarcerated parents or family members, they all have experienced ACEs.

Background of the study

The ACES study was conducted to determine the relationship between childhood experiences and their link to health problems. The original ACES study was conducted in 1995 from the Kaiser Permanente's Appraisal Clinic in San Diego, California.

The most common of the seven categories of childhood exposure was substance abuse in the household. The least common category was criminal exposure. There was a strong relationship between the number of childhood exposures and the number of health-risk factors as the leading cause of death in adults. Risks including smoking, obesity, depression, and suicide increased, as did illicit drug use, sexual intercourse, and sexually transmitted diseases as the number of ACES increased (Felitti et al., 1998).

Since the original 1995-1996 study, Anda, Felitti, and other CDC researchers have published over 60 papers, and their work has been referenced more than 1,500 times (Stevens, 2012). Medical experts have concluded that exposure to ACES has an impact on adult health. "Prevention of the occurrence of ACES, preventing the adoption of health-risk behaviors as responses to ACES during childhood and adolescence, and helping change the health-risk behaviors may alleviate a long-term consequence of ACES" (Felitti et al., 1998, para. 4). Because ACES are common and lead to long-term, health-risk behaviors, prevention strategies are needed.

It was important to address the experiences that children endure, such as sexual, physical, and emotional abuse; substance abuse; parental separation or divorce; and physical and emotional neglect. The exposure to mental illnesses in the household, at an early age, can be problematic (Felitti et al., 1998). It is important to provide safe, nurturing relationships and environments so that students can gain the help to cope with these ACES while in school, especially with the return of all students back to the classroom post-

pandemic. COVID-19 has created its own issues and has also had a lasting impact. Our education system was not ready for COVID-19, especially given the volume of students already struggling with ACES. There needs to be positive interventions to assist and support our students.

To date, some students carry those burdens with them daily. Many students have no one with whom to discuss or share their ACES, especially at home. They have to keep their issues to themselves. Some students are not aware that there are resources that they can use within their school. In some school districts, there are no positive interventions that support students with ACES because most teachers are not aware that their students suffer with the residuals. Even though ACES involve significant health-related issues, it has not been addressed in schools. According to Chicago Public School officials, 30% of students with a personal history of abuse or neglect received an out-of-school suspension during the 2013-2014 school year (Pratt, 2017). If there are ACES-related issues occurring at school, then they need to be managed properly, especially since the COVID-19 pandemic. Too many school districts are without access to ACES-related information needed to help minimize these issues.

Some students commit crimes and get sent to juvenile detention; some students drop out of school. U.S. Senator Dick Durbin (IL) and U.S. Representative Danny Davis (IL) are developing a plan to introduce federal legislation aimed at helping identify and aid children who have experienced violence-induced trauma (Pratt, 2017). Durbin believed that the bill "is part of the solution to the violence we see in our streets here and across the country" (Pratt, 2017, para. 2). According to Chicago Public School officials, 30% of students with a personal history of abuse or neglect received an out-of-school suspension during the 2013-2014 school year (Pratt, 2017).

Lack of support and interventions are significant because students with ACES are likely to have attendance and disciplinary issues in school. Some of the students who suffer ACES are (a) facing expulsion, (b) dropping out of high school, and (c) being led through the juvenile correctional center (Gorman-Smith, & Tolan, 1998). Witnesses or victims of sexual abuse, physical abuse, and child neglect can also suffer high-stress levels and possible depression. If there are no interventions in place to address the effects of ACES for students, then higher rates of health-related issues will occur as they approach adulthood.

When I decided to conduct my own research on ACES, I did it based on my experiences growing up. My dissertation chair told me to choose a topic that I found of interest and that was when I started doing research. At that time, I was the Director of Student Activities at my former school. I also became the mother of the building for some strange reason! Students started to come to me to talk about their life stories or share their stories about them growing up.

I think that's the reason why a lot of students related to me because we shared the same experiences growing up. I realized that I could actually help them because I've already experienced some of the things that they had yet to experience, because I too have ACES. The need to educate and address ACES is at an all-time high. I conducted research because I wanted to see if there was a relationship between ACES scores and participation in extracurricular activities (EA) in high school young adults. The research did show that those students that participated in extracurricular activities were better in school than those that didn't participate in EA.

Extracurricular Activities (EA) are where students enjoy a sense of freedom without academic struggles. An EA is any activity that happens outside of instructional hours in the school setting. Students across the globe participate in various forms of EA that are sports-related such as basketball and cheerleading. EA clubs include student council and speech. Children spend more than half of their waking hours in leisure activities (Eccles, Barber, Stone, & Hunt, 2003). Activities are offered at every level within the school setting; therefore, opportunities are numerous for students to become involved. I watched all kinds of students get together and form special bonds. Basketball players wanted to become actors and band members all at the same time. The reward can be a higher academic performance, peer acceptance, and even social advancement (Eccles et al., 2003).

It is important for those students who can be identified with ACES to get involved with extracurricular activities. EA can promote relationships and environments that help children grow up to be healthy and productive citizens; EA can be used to help build stronger and safer families and communities for all children (CDC, 2016b).

If it wasn't for EA, I don't know where I would be today. Extra-curricular activities saved my life! My parents worked late hours, so the majority of the time, and my siblings were at home raising ourselves. I had the neighborhood Boys and Girls Club to go to. I stayed there every day until it closed at 9 pm. As for my students, I noticed that they all stayed after school to participate in something because they never wanted to go home. Every year I came up with a different program or club that the students brought to me because they just wanted to be at school. They never wanted to go home. When they left their respective activities, they would go and participate in athletics.

Engagement in school-wide EA is linked to decreasing rates of early school dropouts in both boys and girls (Mahoney & Cairns, 1997). Most school dropouts range between the ages of 16-17 years old. I noticed that there was more involvement with the juniors and seniors than the freshman. The students noticed it as well. In one of the clubs, they decided to create a "big brother, little brother" club where they incorporated the freshmen and made them feel welcome. I also noticed that other clubs started doing the same. From our marching band to the cheerleaders, it was an amazing sight to see! EA has also been examined as a means for enhancing school engagement for youth at risk for school dropout (Gilman, Meyers, & Perez, 2004). The benefits of activity participation in reducing problem behaviors are particularly strong among high-risk youth (Eccles et al., 2003).

Supporting an increase in student involvement in activities helped to create safe, supportive relationships amongst the students, which lead to an increase in student achievement, improved student behaviors, and improved attendance. A lot of students did not even realize that I was a special education teacher because I interacted with so many students, ranging from the gifted and talented students to the severely profound. The commonality was student involvement.

After teaching in a high school setting after 18 years, I decided to try my talents at an elementary school. I did not realize at the time that we would still be under COVID-19. However, I was able to teach virtually at an elementary school for the first time. It has definitely been an experience. I have not been able to interact with the students virtually as much as the students in school. However, what I have learned is that they have voluntarily shared the same experiences as my students in high school.

One of my students, who has been frequently absent from school, shared with me her reason for not attending the school or attending virtually. She's in the fifth grade, and the oldest of her siblings, who all attend the school in a different grade. Her grandmother, who she lives with, does not have Wi-Fi for her to attend school virtually. Her grandmother will not allow her or her siblings to walk to school because of the neighborhood that the school is in. Due to circumstances that are out of her control, she has missed out on an important year in school. She won't be at that school next year. She'll be in the sixth grade. Not only does she have ACES, at the rate that she's going, she's likely to become a statistic. COVID-19 also did not help her situation at all. She has to miss school to take care of her siblings because her grandmother was in the hospital. All of that responsibility for a 5th grader during a pandemic cannot possibly be easy.

My transition from high school to elementary was not an easy transition. I noticed during this school year, the school focused on taking the state exam. There were students that never came to school this year or attended virtually take a test that they weren't prepared for. At my former high school, students did not get the choice whether to attend school or participate virtually. School was virtual for all. Imagine the impact on students with ACES during COVID-19. What's going to happen to them? Will they receive the help that they need? Trying to attend school during a worldwide pandemic has been extremely hard for a lot of students. For students with ACES, there already needs to be interventions set up in school. Now that we have to address those same students from the COVID-19 pandemic, there are more interventions, including safety, that need to take place.

Administrators should consider professional development for a better understanding of ACES and COVID-19. While some students are going to be excited to return back to the classroom, some will not. Social-emotional learning and social-emotional support should take the lead in the education curriculum. For example, journal writing or art for students in the classroom are different ways for students to express themselves. Social Promotion of EA, as well as school funding for students K-12 and beyond, should also be considered. Physical Education is considered an EA. Having protective factors such as EA can be beneficial to the staff as well as all students who are faced with adversities. Used as a tool, EA can promote relationships and environments that help children grow up to be healthy and productive citizens.

References

- Burns, J. M., & Szabo, M. (2002, October 7). Depression in young people: What causes it and how can we prevent it? *The Medical Journal of Australia, 177,* 93-96.

- Centers for Disease Control and Prevention [CDC]. (2014, May 4). *About BRFSS.* Retrieved from http://www.cdc.gov/brfss/about/index.htm

- Center for Disease Control and Prevention [CDC]. (2016a, April 1). *About adverse childhood experiences.* Retrieved from http://www.cdc.gov/violenceprevention/acestudy/about_ace.html

- Center for Disease Control and Prevention [CDC]. (2016b, June 14). *About the CDC-Kaiser ACE study.* Retrieved from https://www.cdc.gov/violenceprevention/acestudy/about.html

- Centers for Disease Control and Prevention [CDC]. (2017, Feb 12). *Adverse childhood experiences (ACEs).* Retrieved from http://www.cdc.gov/violenceprevention/acestudy/index.html

- Center for Disease Control and Prevention [CDC]. (2019). *Essentials for childhood: Creating safe, stable, nurturing relationships and environments.* Retrieved from https://www.cdc.gov/violenceprevention/childabuseandneglect/essentials.html

- Eccles, J. S., Barber, B. L., Stone, M., & Hunt, J. (2003). Extracurricular activities and adolescent development. *Journal of Social Issues, 59*(4), 865-889. doi:10.1046/j.0022-4537.2003.00095

- Felitti, V. J., Anda, R. F., Nordenberg, D., Williamson, D. F., Spitz, A. M., Edwards, V., Marks, J. S. (1998). Relationship of childhood abuse and household dysfunction to many of the leading causes of death in adults. *American Journal of Preventive Medicine, 14*(4), 245-258. doi:10.1016/s0749-3797(98)00017-8

- Gilman, R., Meyers, J., & Perez, L. (2004). Structured extracurricular activities among adolescents: Findings and implications for school psychologists. *Psychology in the Schools, 41*(1), 31-41.

- Gorman–Smith, D., & Tolan, P. (1998). The role of exposure to community violence and developmental problems among inner-city youth. *Development and Psychopathology, 10*(1), 101-116.

- Mahoney, J. L. (2014). School extracurricular activity participation and early school dropout: A mixed-method study of the role of peer social networks. *Journal of Educational and Developmental Psychology, 4*(1), 143-156.

- Mahoney, J. L., & Cairns, R. B. (1997). Do extracurricular activities protect against early school dropout? *Developmental Psychology, 33*(2), 241-253. doi:10.1037//0012-1649.33.2.241

- Pratt, G. (2017, March 19). Durbin, Davis push for bill to address childhood trauma. *Chicago Tribune.* Retrieved from https://www.chicagotribune.com/politics/ct-durbin-davis-children-trauma-violence-met-20170318-story.html

- Snyder, T. D., & Dillow, S. A. (2012). *Digest of education statistics 2011.* Washington, DC: National Center for Education Statistics.

- Stevens, J. E. (Ed.). (2012). The adverse childhood experiences study: The largest, most important public health study you never heard of: Began in an obesity clinic. *ACES Too High News*. Retrieved from www.huffpost.com

Dr. Rhonda Richetta
Principal
City Springs Elementary/Middle School, Baltimore, MD

In 2007, City Springs Elementary/Middle School was the first school in the State of Maryland to implement restorative practices, which resulted in a dramatic shift in school climate and reduction in suspensions. Suspensions were reduced from eighty-three in 2007-2008 to ten suspensions in the 2008-2009 school year. Through the implementation of restorative practices, the school's culture was transformed, therefore raising student academic achievement.

In the past fourteen years, City Springs has continued to use restorative practices and has become a model for other schools. This is especially noteworthy considering the population served at City Springs. In 2016, the Abell Foundation released a report that ranked the poverty level of all Baltimore City Public Schools by using the Community Eligibility Provision (CEP). According to this report, City Springs ranked 125 out of 125 elementary schools and 93 out of 93 middle schools.

Rhonda Richetta holds a Bachelor of Science Degree in Education from East Stroudsburg University, a Master of Science Degree in Education from Johns Hopkins University, and a Doctor of Education Degree from Seton Hall University in Education Leadership, Management, and Policy. She continues to serve as the principal of City Springs Elementary/Middle School and lives in Baltimore with her four dogs.

www.citysprings.school

Restorative Practices in Schools: Our Choice or Our Obligation?

By Dr. Rhonda Richetta

Educators have a moral imperative to create school environments where children can thrive emotionally, socially, and academically. This has always been especially pertinent in a school in which the overwhelming majority of children suffer from direct and indirect trauma, which has become an all-to-common side effect of urban poverty, and now, post-pandemic, this will be even more necessary in all schools.

As our youth around this nation are returning to school after a year of missed education, lack of structure, emotional support, and socialization, the challenges facing educators are enormous and the need for restorative environments in schools is more essential now than ever before. In schools, children are expected to follow certain rules, protocols, and social norms. These become routine for children when attending school daily.

Typically, any absence from school or upset in their routine requires teachers to review the rules and even incentivize children to meet the expectations. Educators have come to anticipate these times, such as Monday mornings, the first day after a holiday break, and especially when students return to school after the summer break. The longer the break, the higher the need to reteach expectations and practice routines.

It is common for schools to spend a significant amount of time in the first two weeks of a new school year reviewing rules and social norms and practicing routines, such as hall walking, lining up, and accessing materials. After being home for over a year without having to follow rules and routines and perhaps even experiencing significant loss or trauma during this time, educators will need to set boundaries for students, but provide high support for them to meet these norms.

The Social Discipline Window created by Paul McCold and Ted Wachtel, which is the foundation for restorative practices, provides a tool that pushes educators to think about what supports they can put in place to ensure students will meet high expectations rather than thinking about what consequences they can implement if they do not. Helping students to develop the academic habits and social-emotional skills they will need when they return to school can best be accomplished by using restorative practices.

When I became the principal of an urban Baltimore school fourteen years ago, the state test scores, school culture, and teacher morale had plummeted to an all-time low. There was no doubt in my mind that improving academic outcomes was not going to happen without an environment that was conducive to learning. Doing this in a school where 99 percent of the students qualified for free and reduced meals and the mobility rate was over 30 percent was going to be a colossal task, but I believed that our students had a right to such an environment, and we had an obligation to provide it. I was reminded of the words I heard from my mother over and over my entire life, "I *can't* is not a word in the dictionary."

I heard about restorative practices (RP) for schools from the then president of our charter operator, the Baltimore Curriculum Project. City Springs Elementary/Middle School is a conversion charter school, that is, an existing neighborhood public school that has been converted to a charter school but continues to serve the neighborhood population. Students attend the school by virtue of their address rather than through an application process. Our families are fortunate that their zoned neighborhood school is a charter school.

The president offered to send me to the International Institute for Restorative Practices in Bethlehem, PA, for four days of training in restorative practices. I was open to learning about anything that would help change the culture and climate of our school. My experience in Bethlehem was impactful and convinced me that RP was exactly what our school needed, and I headed back to Baltimore inspired and determined.

I was shocked when not everyone on my staff shared my excitement. I watched the cynical looks on teachers' faces throughout my presentation and when I was finished and asked for questions, the first question asked was, "Does this mean we are not going to suspend kids anymore?" The morale was so low among teachers that they had gotten to a place where their only response to disruptive children was to get rid of them. They had a "zero-tolerance" mindset. They had given up on our kids. They were not motivated to do anything or try anything because they could not see the role that their behavior played in the problem. They saw the children as the problem, therefore, could not buy into the idea that a change in their behavior would make a difference. However, on this initiative, I dug my feet into the sand because I believed that RP could make a difference.

Our initial implementation of restorative practices in 2007 was an arduous, but eventually, a transformational process that involved training of not just teachers and administrators, but all staff — anyone who worked inside the school. After the initial training, there were many skeptics, but I pushed on.

Daily schedules for all students were revised to include "circles" discussions aimed at community building through authentic dialogue. Teachers pushed back, feeling circles were taking away from instructional time. But eventually, the teachers who stayed and bought into RP came to the realization that proactive circles were reaping rewards; classroom culture was transforming throughout the school. Teachers also recognized that the loss of instructional time for circles was less than the loss of instructional time due to behavioral disruptions they had been experiencing. As a leader, resisting the pushback and, instead, providing ongoing support and training was key to our transformation.

The philosophy of restorative practices in schools is simple; *students will do anything for teachers with whom they have strong, positive relationships.* They will be motivated by the relationship, not by any list of rules and consequences hanging on the classroom wall. Trusting relationships are built by giving students a voice and doing things *with* them rather than *to* them or *for* them.

Inappropriate behavior is confronted and what results is decided by all the people affected. Students take responsibility for their behavior and for making things right for the community. The consequence is not predetermined from a menu of consequences focused on simply punishing the behavior, but rather is related to the offense and is focused on replacing the inappropriate behavior with the behavior necessary to have a supportive community.

Critics and resistors will say that RP is permissive, but that is a myth. In a restorative school, wrongdoing and harm is not tolerated. Standards and expectations are high, but so are encouragement and support. There is a deliberate process in place that flows from the proactive methods intended to build a community to the reactive methods to avoid and resolve conflict.

Some mistake student voice for permissiveness or lack of accountability when, in fact, giving students "voice" enables educators to teach replacement behavior and gain insights into the struggles that our children are facing. In such an environment, students thrive, and adults thrive as well.

Even a visit to the principal's office is a very different experience when using restorative practices. Rather than unquestionably assuming guilt in a particular incident by asking the child offender, "Why did you do that?" and immediately moving to discuss the punishment, it starts with the principal asking, "What happened?" and then truly listening to the student's response to that question.

When students feel that an adult is actually listening to and concerned about their side of the story, trust develops and eventually permeates through the entire school community. Students know that a visit to the principal's office may result in consequences of some sort, but they also know that if they have fallen short of the expectations, they will be heard and treated fairly. They know that their behavior will cause disappointment, but not a loss of love, or they know they will be helped to move out of their rage rather than having it intensified.

I once responded to an urgent call for help from a teacher. When I arrived, I found the teacher and students lined up outside the classroom with looks of fear on their faces and a student filled with anger throwing furniture around the classroom. I went into the classroom and calmly asked the student to come with me to my office and he immediately complied. I noticed on our walk to my office his fists were held tight in a ball.

When we got to my office, I told him we would talk about what happened when he was calm and that I was going to finish up my work while he calmed down. I suggested that he breathe and then turned to my computer. Suddenly, I heard the loud sound of sucking in air. I turned to look and saw my student with his eyes closed rhythmically, sucking in long breathes of air and slowly breathing it out. I watched his fists that were rested on the arms of the chair slowly untighten and open up. When they were completely open and relaxed, he opened his eyes, looked at me and said, "Okay, I'm ready to talk now."

It took me a minute to realize that he was using a breathing exercise that we had taught him and one that children do at the beginning of their proactive circles in the classroom daily. He then proceeded to tell me in great detail why he was so angry and how he was feeling. I was completely in awe of how honest and trustful he was able to be with me. I also gained insight into the kind of support I needed to put in place for this child so he could learn to deal with his anger and be successful in school and in life. I thought about how different and unfortunate it would have been for all of us if I had taken a punitive rather than a restorative approach to dealing with this child's unacceptable behavior.

It's that trust—rather than a fear of consequences—that transforms a student's experience in the principal's office or in the classroom, from one of punishment to an experience of understanding and true accountability and respect. The principal and other adults in the school who are trained in restorative practices become sources of motivation and support rather than figures of punishment and fear, which is key to having an impact on our students' futures, and frankly, on the future of our communities. It is also key to having an environment where a sense of urgency about learning can be carried out without significant disruption.

In a restorative school, there can exist a keen focus on academic growth, which, after all, is a school's primary purpose. Trust also comes from the use of consequences that teaches lessons and matches the offenses. We once had a student who did not typically engage in problem behavior, who thought that selling BB's, the pellets for BB guns, in our cafeteria during breakfast was a good way for him to make some money so he could buy snacks for himself and his friends. The staff member who caught him was appalled and suggested that he be suspended immediately. I, on the other hand, chose to use a restorative approach.

As I listened to the student explain why he was selling BB's, I realized that he actually was being quite thoughtful and entrepreneurial. BB guns had become quite popular in our community at this time and his choice of the product he would sell was highly correlated to his environment. I wondered if we were in a community where BB guns were not so popular what he would have chosen to sell. The student and I decided that his consequence would be that he had to arrive to school a half-hour earlier every day and sell fruit snacks to students during breakfast time, the proceeds of which would go to the school, not to him. He was also required to provide me with an income/expense report daily.

The fruit snakes were a hit! The student was surprised to see how quickly a profit could be made. He grew proud of his efforts but was disappointed that the profits were not going to him. When he came and asked me about when he would get to share in the profits, I told him he would not because that was his consequence and his amends to the community he had harmed. However, there was also a lesson and when I asked him what it was, he shared that he learned he could make money by doing something good for the community and it did not have to be something bad. Imagine the impact this approach had on his future compared to the impact of simply suspending him and excluding him from school for a few days.

In Maryland, I sat on a commission that examined the relationship between the school-to-prison pipeline and restorative practices. The school-to-prison pipeline refers to the policies and practices that thrust students out of school and into the criminal justice system, which all too often is the result of exclusionary discipline, such as suspensions and expulsions. Exclusionary discipline is what restorative practices in schools aim to avoid. Exclusionary discipline unfairly impacts students of color. Exclusionary discipline is harming our society by contributing to the school-to-prison pipeline.

We must find a way to provide environments in *all* of our schools that are restorative. We must stop having schools contribute to the violence, crime, and hate that exists in our communities. This should not be something we choose to do. This is something we are obligated to do.

Shawana Thompson
High School English Teacher

Shawana Thompson is a passionate secondary English educator living her childhood dream of being an educator. Her love for teaching and mentorship is seen through her interaction with her students as she finds innovative ways to connect with them and build a lasting relationship they will never forget.

Shawana has a BA in English and a Master of Science in Human Service Administration. Her background includes project accounting as well as support admin for high-level executives. Shawana lives in Maryland and enjoys reading, running, and spending time with her son.

Sthompson3114@gmail.com

Instagram: @journeyspurposeinc

Inclusion Conclusion

By Shawana Thompson

Education is one of the most rewarding fields one can work in. However, it has evolved over time and this has changed the dynamics of the classroom. Some of the changes have been positive and aligned with our ever-changing world, such as having technology in the classroom easily accessible to students and educators. Other changes include inclusion, which is something I find very challenging.

Inclusion, simply stated, is the acceptance of students with disabilities into a general educational classroom with students without disabilities. According to the Individuals with Disabilities Education Act (IDEA), students with special needs have the right to receive necessary curricular adaptations. Adaptations include accommodations and modifications (Special Education Guide, 2021). If students with disabilities are in a general education classroom, then the expectation is that they will be held to the academic standards as their peers. However, their accommodations have modifications that lower the expectations and this is problematic for the student, educator, and peers.

Inclusion in the general education classroom for students with disabilities has been a long-standing controversial topic. It has been enforced for many years by various entities. IDEA advocates for students with disabilities to be included. Before IDEA, however, the Regular Education Initiative (REI) was first presented. REI placed most students with mild disabilities in general classrooms to be taught by general educators (Shade & Stewart, 2001).

Essentially, inclusion means that the student with special education needs is attending the general school program, enrolled in age-appropriate classes 100% of the school day (Idol, 2006). Inclusion is a sensitive and layered topic within the education system. Inclusion can range from students with speech impediments to students with classic autism. One student with a disability may not require the same level of accommodation as another student with a disability. While the inclusion topic is controversial, teacher feedback and classroom experiences have shown that inclusion is ineffective and not healthy for the students overall.

As an educator, I have taught classes with a co-teacher and classes without co-teachers. Co-teachers are special education teachers who are in the room as a resource for the students with special needs. The design is for the content teacher to teach the lesson and the special education teacher to assist students with disabilities and add differentiation to the lessons. Each co-teacher relationship is different depending on the level of experience and education of the content and co-teachers. Here are two scenarios about my experience and why I am not an advocate of inclusion.

Scenario 1

I am an English teacher and I teach ninth graders, primarily. I had a class of approximately 24-26 students. Most of those in the class were reading at a fourth to fifth-grade level. I also had students who were classic cases of autism and some students who were classified with Attention Deficit Hyperactivity Disorder (ADHD). One student's autism was more severe and it involved sensory issues with a heightened sense of anxiety in spaces where things could change.

This student would yell out and make noises during the entire class period. Every day, my co-teacher and I would have to remove the student because she was a distraction. Other students would yell out "shut up" or "stop" and other phrases that disrupted class, which made the student with autism more anxious and louder. If my co-teacher removed the student from the room, I was then left in the classroom with all 24 students who were below reading level, had difficulty staying on task, and some would not do work unless I was literally sitting beside them and coaching them.

One teacher in a room full of students with various special education needs is problematic for many reasons. First, one teacher cannot possibly cater to the needs of a classroom of 24 students, especially when eleven of them have an Individualized Learning Plan (IEP) or a 504 plan. IEP's and 504's are legal documents that require educators to adhere to the accommodations put in place by the IEP team. The co-teacher for this class was experienced and organized. However, the student made it difficult for us to thrive as teachers.

Scenario 2

I had another class that was a co-taught class. The class had about two to three IEP's along with some very immature boys who often created distractions with their outbursts and behavior. Honestly, they were boys being boys, but having to stop teaching to address their behavior often resulted in the class being disrupted.

My co-teacher for this class was a new special education teacher on a provisional special education license. She was attending school while teaching, which meant she had no experience and was showing up every day expecting to assist me in ensuring that special education students were given proper accommodations. I felt alone and overwhelmed because, on paper, I am, as the content teacher, completely responsible for all students' learning and classroom management.

Special education teachers should be able to help differentiate lesson plans so that all learners grasp the lesson concepts. They should also help manage classroom behaviors and issues. None of that was happening, which caused extra stress for me. When asked, the co-teacher said she was still learning and did not really know what to do.

The reason both scenarios are problematic is because inclusion created an environment that became more distracting and ultimately caused both the special needs students and the students without disabilities to suffer. In each class scenario, one set of students and or the educators were being shortchanged. Neither I nor my students were getting the necessary support to be successful. Another reason these scenarios are problematic is that the frustration of the teacher stems from the overwhelming task of adhering to the needs of the student with the disability as well as the needs of the other students in the classroom.

In a study about teachers' perspective on inclusion, teachers considered resource rooms for special needs students an effective delivery system. Most believed students with mild disabilities could not be effectively educated entirely in the general classroom, even with instructional support. They believed that resource room programs should be increased and expanded to better serve those students in need of special education services (Shade & Stewart, 2001). The attitude of educators is critical when considering inclusion and should be assessed often. Inclusionary practices may be defeated if general education teachers do not have positive attitudes toward these practices (Shade & Stewart, 2001).

Inclusion sounds good in theory and parents have fought for their children with special needs to be included in general education classrooms. They feel it allows students with disabilities to interact with students who do not have disabilities and connects them with social interaction activities. Research shows children with disabilities should learn and play alongside their non-disabled peers (Fuchs & Fuchs, 1998). While I completely understand where parents are coming from and agree that students should interact with students without disabilities, I am more inclined to consider other ways to socially acclimate the students outside the classroom.

Social-emotional learning is critical for the development of students with disabilities. However, the negative impact it has on the students without and with the disability is too great. When special educators cannot meet the need in the classroom as a resource, it discourages the student with the disability as they cannot effectively learn without the help provided. Further, I'm positive parents would not be happy to witness disruptions that are so great, their students are prevented from quality education. I've been observed and heard comments about how the disruptions are painful. However, nothing changed. It's a hindrance for all parties involved.

Social justice is a grounding principle of inclusion since it supports respect, care, recognition, and empathy and challenges beliefs as well as practices that directly or indirectly encourage the continuation of marginalization and exclusion (Obiakor et al., 2012). Being adequately trained should be a prerequisite for general education teachers. Some progress is being made in preparing general educators for the eventuality of educating exceptional needs students in the regular classroom; however, that progress is slow in coming and far from complete (Shade & Stewart, 2001).

Unfortunately, slow progress of training for a need that is critical is not enough. When general educators are not properly trained, the students suffer because they are not getting what they need to succeed. When teachers are not trained properly, they may feel less confident in their ability to teach the special needs student as well as deal with behavior issues that come along with students with disabilities. Another reason the practice of inclusion does not measure up to the theory is because of the critical shortage of special education teachers in the United States.

Special education teachers are supposed to assist the general educator in the classroom with the students who have disabilities. If there is a shortage, school districts are forced to hire potentially under-qualified individuals because having a special educator is required. This shortage is chronic and severe and exists in every geographic region of the nation. The number of special education teachers nationally has dropped by more than 17 percent over the past decade. For the 2015-16 school year, which offers the most up-to-date data, there was one special education teacher for every 17 students with disabilities. That's more special education students per special educator than the overall teacher-student ratio, which has held steady at about 1 to 16 for the past decade (Samuels, 2019).

In closing, inclusion is not effective because the students with the disability, the students without disabilities, and the teacher all suffer. Unfortunately, inclusion seems to solely rest on the shoulders of educators and that is not fair to us. In fact, it is unfair for the students with special needs who are not getting the high individualized support to which they are legally entitled. The system is designed for the students to fail academically at the expense of them being included socially. Inclusion should not be a one-man job but a community offering solutions that will be in the best interest of the student.

As an advocate for a high-quality education for all students, I would recommend that the current practice of inclusion be evaluated in-depth and remodeled to provide students and educators with a solid practice that works. The practices to be considered as a classroom teacher would be parents visiting the class on a regular basis to witness and see what transpires daily. Additionally, special education teachers should be required to earn a dual certification in specific content areas so they are familiar with the content and can teach the special needs population in an engaging way that promotes learning.

Special education teachers that are dually certified could be a better resource for students and could possibly teach in a more secluded space that may not be a part of general education so that students with disabilities are able to experience the help and instruction they need without distraction. All students deserve a quality education and the very best of their educators through meaningful instruction. The current inclusion model is non-effective due to unqualified staff, burnout, and disruptions at the cost of social inclusion.

References

- Fuchs, D., & Fuchs, L. S. (1998). Competing visions for educating students with disabilities: Inclusion versus full inclusion. *Childhood Education, 74*(5), 309-316. Retrieved from https://goucher.idm.oclc.org/login?url=https://search-proquest-com.goucher.idm.oclc.org/docview/210393339?accountid=11164

- Idol, L. (2006). Toward inclusion of special education students in general education: A program evaluation of eight schools: RASE TL & LD. *Remedial and Special Education, 27*(2), 77-94. doi:http://dx.doi.org.goucher.idm.oclc.org/10.1177/07419325060270020601

- McLeskey, J., Tyler, N. C., & Susan, S. F. (2004). The supply of and demand for special education teachers: A review of research regarding the chronic shortage of special education teachers. *The Journal of Special Education, 38*(1), 5-21. doi:http://dx.doi.org.goucher.idm.oclc.org/10.1177/00224669040380010201

- Obiakor, F. E., Harris, M., Mutua, K., Rotatori, A., & Algozzine, B. (2012). Making inclusion work in general education classrooms. *Education & Treatment of Children, 35*(3), 477-490. Retrieved from https://goucher.idm.oclc.org/login?url=https://search-proquest-com.goucher.idm.oclc.org/docview/1024808071?accountid=11164

- Richard A. Shade & Roger Stewart (2001) General Education and Special Education Preservice Teachers' Attitudes Toward Inclusion, Preventing School Failure: Alternative Education for Children and Youth, 46:1, 37-41, DOI: 10.1080/10459880109603342

- Samuels, Christina. (2019). The shrinking number of special ed teachers adds to schools' pressures. https://www.pbs.org/newshour/education/the-shrinking-number-of-special-ed-teachers-adds-to-schools-pressure

Gerald Moore
STEM Educator

Mr. Moore is a powerful speaker who uses his story as an at-risk youth to change the narrative for disadvantaged and underserved students. He teaches how he overcame being a low-achieving student to working for top consulting firms in the world. He leverages his experience with racism in corporate America as a diversity and inclusion speaker focusing on how to discuss race in the workplace.

Mr. Moore is a graduate of Norfolk State University, where he achieved a degree in Electronics Engineering Technology. He has over 20 years of experience as a federal government contractor as an information Technology and Cybersecurity Engineer. He has also worked as an educator in the public school system teaching technology.

He is a two-time Amazon Best Selling Author, most noted for his first title, "Motivate Black Boys - How to Prepare for Careers in STEM." He is also the founder of Mission Fulfilled 2030, a non-profit organization and Technology School for Black boys. He has been featured by many media outlets and publications such as Black Enterprise, NBC, Sirius Radio, iHeart, and Washington Times.

www.missionfufilled2030.org

Technology is the Future of Education

By Gerald Moore

F ire all the teachers! Gone are the days of antiquated classrooms with one teacher standing in front of a black or white board dictating information to students seated quietly in straight rows. The future of education rests on teachers' ability to incorporate technology in all facets of teaching and offer global learning experiences to children across the wordl. But, do I really think that all teachers should be fired? No! But most should.

In a world that has proven to be unpredictable, a global pandemic is something the majority of the world had not planned for. But it has provided us with some very valuable lessons regarding our educational systems here in the United States. The COVID-19 pandemic has shown us that we were not technologically prepared to pivot and provide continuity of operations for our national education system. In that, we are failing one of the country's most precious resources, our students. I believe the pandemic has uncovered one of the many weaknesses of our school system, and unfortunately, one of the biggest happens to be teacher preparation and efficacy.

As an independent STEM educator, I am always trying to work with school administration and teachers to keep them abreast of new technology and how they can leverage new and emerging technological resources within and beyond the classroom environment. It was no surprise to me that school districts in mass were not equipped or positioned to pivot in response to having to shut schools down. Though I cannot fault them for the initial response to shutdowns, hopefully, we have learned from this unfortunate incident that we can never go back to school business as usual. We must take this opportunity to implement education reform that is necessary for the betterment of our public education system.

In my interactions with teachers as we entered this new normal of asynchronous or remote learning during the pandemic, I began to realize that the teachers were hesitant to learn new technology or felt overwhelmed by being forced to adapt to the situation at hand. From my perspective, I feel like it exposed the limitations of teachers' ability to respond to change, which is a major part of creating a system that is ahead of the curve.

I believe that our teachers should, at a minimum, be open to opportunities to gain knowledge and transition our education system in any way necessary to benefit the students. This is an asset to their skill set. The number of teachers that I spoke with who were unwilling to learn or resistant to embrace the new changes is still amazing to me. Yes, sometimes change is difficult, but the only thing that is constant is change.

Having had the opportunity to be an in-classroom instructor in the high school and middle school setting in a Title I school district, I have a tremendous amount of respect for what teachers have to endure. But at the same time, I believe that being a teacher is a calling and those that are called should be willing to do what's necessary to fulfill that calling with minimum resistance. Those who are not called should take the opportunity to exit or stop fighting the inevitable and adapt to this new education paradigm.

Based on my experience, as a student and as an educator, I have firsthand knowledge of why we need to have a change in education. Going back as a young Black male in school, I was a poor student, not because I couldn't grasp concepts, but the system never fit who I was as a student. Black men make up less than 2% of the public school workforce. I never had a black male educator my entire K through 12 experience and having a black man in my educational path would have made a significant difference.

This significance has been proven for me by the mere fact that remote education teachers have been able to bring me into their virtual classrooms and then talk to me, afterward, about the impact that I have had on their students. This is especially true for, but certainly not limited to, students of color. Now we know that representation matters. This new forced virtual education model presents the opportunity to bridge the gap by bringing more Black men into the classroom and providing that representation for young Black boys who need it.

As a student, I never understood why I couldn't learn the types of things that I wanted to learn, like electronics and design. I spent a tremendous amount of time learning about electronics and design outside of school and was failing in school because I was disinterested in the subject matter and rarely had a teacher that could motivate and engage me as a student.

I graduated college with a degree in Electronics Engineering Technology. I began working with youth while in college, after experiencing my first encounter with racism while working for an electronics company in an internship program where I did not receive a comparable title or salary with my white male counterparts even though I scored significantly higher on the companies engineering aptitude test, which was supposed to determine placement, in the company. I was hired with the title of Senior Technician while my white male counterparts became Engineers.

The difference in salary was about $15,000 and an additional week's vacation. I resigned immediately, recognizing that as the only Black person in the division, I would never be treated fairly and refused to start my career this way. I realized that my ability to educate, activate and motivate youth in technology was something that came naturally for me. When the opportunity presented itself to teach electronics technology at my high school alma mater, I jumped on the opportunity as I thought that I could add value to students and faculty.

As I began this journey as a young educator, I learned that all students were entitled to their own Individualized Education Plan (IEP). But what happens is that the only children that end up with their own IEP, specifically tailored for them, are those who are deemed special needs based on a disability. I can see now, as an educator, why I needed a customized learning plan based on learning assets, not learning deficits.

I was a D student in school, but I would score really high on all my state-mandated testing. I got in trouble a lot in school. I remember being in meetings where they would reference my test scores and say, "Gerald is in the highest percentile in his New York state test scores, but it's just not transitioning to the classroom. Maybe he's not being challenged."

Nobody ever thought to ask me, what is it that I wanted to learn? And it wasn't until I was on the verge of being expelled from school that a social worker asked me, "What can we do to help you do better in school?" It was at that point; I finally had the opportunity to discuss the types of things I wanted to learn and all of the work that I was doing outside of school.

I was an engineer at ten years old. I was always tinkering and building and designing and developing. But that wasn't a part of my curriculum at school, and nobody ever asked me about my interests. The response to my academic ability regarding my testing was always, "Maybe he's not being challenged." The solution was to give me more of the same work at a higher level as though that was going to work for me. It didn't. And it doesn't work for most students.

What we have with technology today is the opportunity to bridge the gap in education and provide students with a truly Individualized Education Plan that can meet each student's specific needs and interests. But if our teachers are not willing to learn new technology and be able to deliver new technology to the children that need a different program, then those teachers need to be removed from the education system. Otherwise, the system will continue to fail students.

One of the high school students I mentor said to me one day during the mentoring session, "What's the purpose of public-school education? I don't get it, like, I don't get to do anything that inspires me toward my career goals. All we do is work on prepping for the state-mandated tests." My response to him was, "Let's look it up." Here is what we found.

According to the National School Boards Association (NSBA, public education exists to serve this purpose: *Prepare students for college and the workforce, including preparing them for jobs that may not even exist yet due to rapidly changing technology.* If this is the case, we are in utter failure. In our inner cities, most of our children are not prepared for college. And they're not prepared for the workforce, either.

Our schools haven't done well in transitioning and preparing for those jobs in the future that don't even exist. As a technology professional, I question how we prepare students for the workforce of the future when we know that technology is the workforce of the future, and yet, we don't have any technology professionals in our school buildings.

Part two of the purpose, as indicated by NSBA, is to *help our children fulfill their diverse potentials.* Our school systems are definitely not doing this. We spend most of our time working on the mastery of the common core curriculum. And most children, like myself as a youth, and a lot of my students now never get to explore the things they really want to learn and the things they feel are important to them.

I also believe that our schools, especially in our inner cities, are failing our children as the majority of the curriculum is not culturally relevant. The majority of our teachers in Title I school districts are middle-aged white females who do not share or understand the lived experiences of black and brown children. They don't understand that education needs to be culturally relevant and many of them don't know how to provide it.

Therefore, when it comes down to accommodating the diverse potential of students, schools are not meeting the mark. Most aren't even aware of students' diverse potential.

Part three of the purpose of education reads: *Enable students to become well-rounded*

individuals, focusing on the whole child, and not just mastery of the academic content. As my student pointed out, what we see in our public schools is most of the time being spent working on mastery of random content in preparation for the state-mandated testing.

I think we're seeing a shift in the workforce and the disruption of the education system, especially in the technology sector, because many major companies in the high-tech digital industry are saying that the school system is not preparing students for the workforce. Therefore, they are now taking an active role in creating their own programming for the development of their workforce.

What the pandemic of 2020 has taught us is that our school systems are not prepared for the future. But the disruption of the education system is upon us, and it will be those in the technology sector who will be the new leaders of the education system. I am now a part of that community. As a technology educator, I have the ability to educate the masses from a remote location.

Digital technology educators have the ability to impact student learning and provide students with more diverse education options. Digital technology educators have the capacity to pivot quickly and create educational products most teachers cannot create within the confines of the current system. We must embrace these new opportunities and bypass the bureaucracy of a school system that continues to fail our children.

American students are continuously lagging behind in most of the technology categories. We also lag behind in entrepreneurship, engineering, and math. The only way that we're going to be able to catch up is that we add new educational options within the school system and leverage the technology at hand. We must then bring forth people who can adapt to new ways of thinking and teaching so they/we can provide more opportunities for students to participate through individualized education programs designed to meet their needs.

Our Generation Z children have grown up with the internet. They've grown up with Google, Instagram, YouTube, and other social media apps that are actually a part of their personal operating system. Technology is how they communicate, learn, and interact. Our teachers are like PCs and our Gen Z students are like Apple and Mac devices. It is as if teachers are trying to install their outdated PC software into our new Apple students. This will not work. They are totally incompatible.

There is a lot of work that needs to be done and I don't believe our Title I schools are equipped to make the immediate changes we need to see as we are transitioning to this post-pandemic educational system. But I know one thing; the disruption of education is upon us. And there are people like me, who have educational organizations that are built on technology. Mission Fulfilled 2030 is here and ready to disrupt the system and provide education for our young people that the schools are not ready to provide.

School districts must be willing to create partnerships with outside organizations that are equipped to provide services they cannot. The education new normal must be one that is truly culturally relevant in a way that is futuristic and not limiting students. Given the ongoing political debate over education reform and the bureaucracy at every level of today's education system, I don't see progress happening with any rate of significance.

The world is rapidly changing, the global economy is accelerating, and the education system holds fast to its traditional ways of schooling. Our antiquated school system must be disrupted in an effort to create opportunities for technology experts and service providers to better serve our students.

As leaders of the future, the technology sector can equip students with the types of education that will meet the workforce demand of the future and provide diverse educational opportunities for them to explore and maximize their abilities.

Denise Newsome
Math and Science Educator

Denise R. Newsome is an educational innovator and entrepreneur. She has nine years of teaching experience in high school science and mathematics. Currently, she is teaching honors chemistry and physics. She is the founder of Focused Educational Solutions, Inc, a STEM tutoring, and consulting company. Her dream is to create an educational system that provides ALL students equal access to STEM education which teaches students the foundational skills required for success in STEM post-secondary education and beyond!

In 2008, she graduated with bachelor's degrees in biochemistry and chemistry with minors in biology and mathematics from Florida State University. She earned her Master of Education in Curriculum and Instruction with an emphasis in Science Education K-14 in 2014 from Concordia University. She is working towards a master's degree in biochemistry at the University of Saint Joseph.

Instagram and Twiiter: @msnewsomenotes

Transformation of Rural STEM Education

By Denise Newsome

It is not the critic who counts, not the man who points out how the strong man stumbles, or where the doer of deeds could have done them better. The credit belongs to the man who is actually in the arena.

–Theodore Roosevelt

My school is a rural PK-12 school in the northern part of my county. One can quickly identify that you are in a rural location when the only fast food readily available is from a gas station. For various reasons, rural schools commonly do not provide strong STEM education due to a lack of resources and highly qualified teachers. When I arrived at my school five years ago, Advanced Placement (AP) science courses had never been offered. I taught the first ever AP Chemistry class and honors physics course offered at my school. More than anything, I wanted to improve the quality of science education offered at my school. I quickly learned that getting my students to pass an AP exam was going to be an insurmountable challenge. A school's culture matters when it comes to getting students to perform well on AP level exams. At the end of my second year, I made the conclusion that outside influencer was needed to help me shift the mindsets of everyone at my school—both students, teachers, and administration.

Through one of the trainings I attended for AP Chemistry, I connected with a colleague from my school district who had connections to a university professor who was on a mission to change the educational landscape of Northwest Florida. He wanted all our students to have access to high-quality STEM education. This connection fostered the partnership between a university professor and a high school teacher who would make a move to change rural STEM education.

In February of 2020, the University Professor drove an hour and a half to offer me a position to work with the Nuclear Medicine and Science Camp in July. I was honored to have been chosen for this opportunity. Being the lead high school teacher would help me to sharpen my knowledge of nuclear science and bring this knowledge back to my students. When all schools were shut down due to COVID-19, it became obvious face-to-face summer camps would not be an option. We were faced with a decision to take the camp online or not have the camp at all. My first thought was we must figure out how to still offer the camp on an online platform because my students need to have access to a unique STEM experience as part of laying the foundation for skills needed for success in STEM college majors. The question then became, "Why not go online?" Students are still going to be "stuck" at home all summer and we had an opportunity to do something that no one had attempted before with a Nuclear Science Camp. There was a chance that the camp would not work out, but we had to exhaust all paths to get this camp online for the sake of keeping students in the STEM pipeline.

There were several key things we had to figure out for this camp to be a success: How do we make the camp "hands-on," how do we engage students online, and how do we get the students to access the spectrometers remotely? Thankfully, the University had funds that needed to be spent on student outreach due to the summer research program being canceled. The funds were invested in the STEM pipeline to support the creation of hands-on Nuclear Science Boxes and additional spectrometers. The University expenditure not only supported this camp, but in the outreach to students from low-socioeconomic status from rural areas. In the rural part of my county and the counties that surround me, students typically do not have access to robust high school STEM programs that help students build the foundational skills required for success in STEM majors and beyond.

The most time-consuming preparation for the camp was getting the spectrometers online so that our students could operate them remotely. This involved over two months of working with IT and figuring out how to get our campers' university accounts to engage in our online environment. At the time of planning, zoom did not have a function to give remote control of the screen. Microsoft teams did offer the remote-control option, but only allowed for one student at a time to control the screen. We wanted each camper in the rotation to control the spectrometers simultaneously. This required an innovation beyond what we currently had access to.

The IT team began working with us on two options — using programs that are typically used for remote access to computers from one location to another and using a university program that allowed for remote access to lab equipment called Virtual Lab. In the testing of the remote access option, we crashed my computer. The remote access option proved to be very cumbersome. After all the testing, the best option was to get all six spectrometers attached to the Virtual Lab.

The Virtual Lab option was not without its challenges. We needed to obtain official university accounts for the students. The only way to get the students' accounts was to go through the Human Resources Department and have the parents "apply" to the University as employees. This proved to be cumbersome and caused us to lose one student due to the confusion of having to become an "employee" of the university.

As with any challenge, there is always an opportunity. The discussion of what to do to make this process less cumbersome and more accessible to all students. Meetings after the camp lead to a discussion on creating developing student accounts to help with furthering the mission of keeping students in the STEM pipeline. From the challenges we faced getting students online, we discovered the need to create "developing student accounts" to provide access to online enrichment opportunities like this. These developing students accounts could also prepare the way for helping to track students into the STEM pipeline. We must seek ways to break down barriers for students to gain access to University systems.

I cannot go into all the details of preparing for this camp, without telling you what we did every day.

Day 1

The Nuclear Camp Team, The Professor, my colleague, STEM Institute Director and I prepared diligently for this day for months. Now it was time to do what we prepared for. At

9:00 am, we had a line of cars to pick up STEM Boxes. At 11 am, we went live with our first zoom session. We began by introducing everyone and allowed the students to introduce themselves. Then we opened the boxes together and got the students prepared for the first investigation. We wanted to get the students comfortable with the contents of the box before we did the first structured activity.

The first hands-on activity of the camp was exploring the intensity of counts vs. distance from the radioactive source. For this activity, we use the Geiger Counter, ruler and radioactive source from the box. Students used the ruler to measure the distance from the source in centimeters and recorded the intensity values in milliRems from the radiation monitor. Students then proceeded to graph by hand the Intensity vs. Distance. The goal was to help students see the relationship and notice it is related to a mathematical principle — the inverse square law. In the 2020 camp, we incorporated an introduction to Google sheets. We wanted to help students get comfortable with the concept of using a spreadsheet as this will be an important skill to acquire before college.

Day 2

On Day 2, we divided the students by their grade levels and kept the Nuclear Science theme. We split the students into three groups — alpha, beta, and gamma. We needed to separate students by grades to be able to guide the discussion based upon the ability levels of each student. Grouping the students into breakout rooms allowed for more in-depth discussion, which was the key design of day 2.

In each box, there was a set of absorbers made of various materials which could potentially attenuate the emission of gamma rays. The radioactive source in each box was not all the same. We had the students test the emission of gamma rays when placing an absorber on top of the source. Using their Geiger counter and radioactive source, the students were able to measure the gamma ray intensity and compare it with the other students in their group. We had one student that went through all of the absorbers and still measure counts. She asked, "Why am I not getting a decrease in counts?" We asked what source she had, and she said Cobalt-60! The 1 MeV gamma rays emitted from Co-60 are not attenuated significantly with the set of absorbers given to the students. This allowed for a more enriched discussion of materials that can attenuate various levels of gamma radiation.

Flip Grid is a popular educational technology tool used by many teachers around the world. It allows for students to upload short, personalized videos on a topic assigned by an educator. We wanted the students to explore their surroundings to determine if they could discover any sources of naturally occurring radioactivity. We were able to see the personalities of the students come out in the Flip Grid videos.

We concluded the day with two virtual field trips. One was to a national laboratory and the other was to a local nuclear medicine facility.

Day 3

Day 3 began with a lesson on Nuclear Spectroscopy and followed with one of our culminating hands-on activities—

remotely operating a PASCO Advanced Nuclear Spectroscopy System. We kept our students in the alpha, beta, and gamma groups for three rotations. Topics included a deep dive into isotopes and radioactivity with the professor, a meeting with college admissions officers and a rotation with my colleague and I on the spectrometers. I wish we had recorded what we looked like running between instruments switching out radioactive sources. From this spectroscopy experience, we were able to introduce students to the concepts of calibrating lab instruments and the unique spectrums generated from different radioactive sources. Spectroscopy is typically an advanced topic. However, our students got it! We must never underestimate what our students are capable of learning with all of the right supports and an engaging learning environment.

Day 4

On the final day of the camp, we concluded with a guest lecture on astrophysics. One of the students in the camp wanted to pursue a career in astrophysics, so this topic was of particular interest to her. We have asked her to return to camp this year as a student assistant. After the final talk and debrief with the students, the boxes were returned and students were awarded a certificate for completing the camp.

Outcomes

My colleague and I had the opportunity to give a talk titled, "A Collaboration Between K-12 Teachers and a University Professor."

This camp would not have been possible without everyone on our team working together in collaboration. The professor brought his expertise as a physicist and the funding to support this endeavor. We all connected over our mission to reach students in a rural area and help them make it all the way through the STEM pipeline.

In the midst of all the work of creating this camp, the university professor messaged me with this crazy idea of starting a Nuclear Medicine and Science Program at my school. The Capstone of this program would be creating a DE course that would be unique to our school and offer credit at a major university, not through a community college. As much as we would love to get every student into Nuclear Science, the mission of the program would be greater than that. Statistically, students who do not take the sequence of biology, chemistry, physics, and calculus do not succeed in the completion of a STEM major. This is particularly true for those from disadvantaged backgrounds. I have pushed for a long time at my school to have a set sequence of courses for our STEM students, but I have been met with challenges. Using the framework of an academy and the support of a university professor might be the key to successful STEM preparation at my school. The academy has been approved. Now we have to see if we can affect change. I have hope that with the support of a university professor, we can fully prepare our students for STEM career success!

In order to make improvements in rural STEM education, we need more programs like this and more university professors who are willing to work in collaboration with K-12 educators to provide quality science education in both primary and secondary schools. We must partner together in this arena to fight for what we know can set our students up for success beyond the K-12 system.

Dr. Natoya Coleman
High School Principal

Dr. Natoya Coleman is a high school administrator who recently graduated from Rowan University with a Ph.D. in Urban and Diverse Learning Environments. With a research focus on the leadership practices of Black female educational leaders within urban and diverse settings, she is particularly interested in theorizing and naming the practices of Black women that are embedded within the fabric of their identity.

She has 14 years of teaching and leadership experience in Secondary Education, and a particular interest in the practical application of theory within the school setting. Currently, she is an Assistant Principal in Flint, Michigan, where she focuses on school culture and climate and student voice.

www.drnatoyacoleman.com

My 16-Day Principalship Practice

By Dr. Natoya Coleman

I t was Friday, and I was at the grocery store picking up my contribution to the festivities of the evening with the school secretary. Terry was gifted a charcuterie board for Christmas, and we had been planning to get together to put it to use since we returned from Winter break. Finally, the day had come, and we were sitting, snacking, and the laughter could be heard several doors down when I received the notification of an email that would change my life.

"Please be informed of the revised reporting structure. Effective immediately, you will serve as 'Acting' Principal until further notice." Terry could see the dread on my face, as I read the email. "Until further notice." Those words were troubling, but despite how I felt, I had two days to gather myself and prepare for leading our building.

It was my very first year as assistant principal. I was still learning and hoping to stay in the role as long as necessary to amass the experiences needed before entering into a principalship. And now, in the middle of a global pandemic, I was thrust into the principalship without warning, indefinitely. Just a few minutes later, my principal began texting me a barrage of things that needed to be done in the coming days, in preparation to receive students back into the building.

Our district was approaching ten months of distance learning, and we were planning to receive students back into the building in one month. Among the tasks placed in my hands were: finalize the COVID-19 building protocols, assemble the COVID-19 planning team, finalize numbers of in-person, distance, and virtual learning students, finalize bus routes, submit lunch counts, secure cleaning supplies and personal protection gear for staff, ensure regular communication with the school community, request deep cleaning of classrooms before the arrival of students, confirm arrangements with building maintenance for daily deep cleaning, and more.

The tasks before me weren't daunting, but the real challenge would be interpersonal. The staff members who I would be leading would eventually become but were not yet *my people*. Leading in a small district is about much more than leadership acumen, but also involves the historical connections and bonds that are established among friends who attend the same church, graduated from the same or rival high schools, taught side by side for 10, 15, 20 years, and who simply prefer working with someone who came from the same town.

My reality was that I was an outsider, and that was a wedge between me and the staff that could not be reversed. We didn't have enough time to forge relationships that make soften the blows of sharing difficult information. Another undeniable reality was the racial dissimilarity between myself and most of the staff, which is white, and I am black. My principal, a white male, already had relationships with many of the staff members, and was well received. The staff loved him because he was "one of us," a former middle school teacher within the district and a graduate of the district. Although I didn't have any overt instances related to race, there was a tension in the building that could not be ignored.

With a history of many outsiders coming in with the initiative to "fix" the district, the teachers and administrators who have stood the test of time are highly regarded, regardless of their instructional and leadership practice. All these factors led to a great conflict within me. I knew that I had the skills to complete the task, but I was fearful of how successful I would be with a low likelihood of gaining the support of the staff.

This concern was confirmed after my first communication ruffled the feathers of some of the veteran staff. While providing instructions on COVID-19 protocols, I used the word "admonish" to remind teachers to wear masks and social distance. This language was met with great disdain and I immediately received text messages and emails with concerns. One of those came from a veteran teacher, a white woman, who kindly offered to proofread my emails in the future to ensure that my language will not anger staff.

My first few days were spent working on the tasks assigned by my principal and answering questions of concern regarding the whereabouts of our leader. With little guidance from central office administration, I went on to do what I could to prepare our school for the return of students in a little less than a month.

In the next 16 days, I initiated our team's COVID-19 Planning team, finalized the building COVID-19 Protocols, prepared student lists, student schedules, bus routes, breakfast and lunch procedures, managed personnel challenges, and more, successfully. Not one day did I need to be rescued or redeemed by central office administration, and not one time did we need to revise or reorganize our plan when students returned to the building. All the staff members and central administration can and will confirm that my leadership was solid and successful, but not without tears.

A leader must be decisive, but the decision must be made with as much insight from others as possible. Decisions made in a vacuum will likely not be supported by the staff and/or administrative team. The principal has the authority to make decisions independently but must understand that the ensuing success depends on the staff following through with the directive.

Such solidarity is not automatic. Leaders must create a community where the most critical leaders are in support of the decisions that are made. This is best done by shared decision-making. This is also done by always making the assumption that the leaders who support the school have valuable insight.

Personal stability was critical for success as a building leader. I found myself spending time over the weekend dealing with my fears, insecurities, and personal struggles so that they did not hinder my ability to think creatively, hear from my colleagues, seek the advice of those who were experienced and supportive in the staff, and defer to those who were more knowledgeable of the district while dealing with various circumstances.

I had to eliminate my need to be the answer, the savior, and I needed to use the resources that were placed around me. This is something that I saw my mentor do, and I understood it with greater depth during my 16 days as a principal. So, I had to encourage myself, affirm myself, and remind myself that I don't have anything to prove. I just need to do what is best for my students.

This self-work allowed me to make sure that I was not in the way, as I led the building. It was humbling and rewarding and is nothing that I learned in my leadership program: that being emotionally healthy would be critical to my success as a building leader. The greatest change that COVID-19 brought for me was my perspective of student success.

Teacher evaluations and student achievement on standardized tests are what characterize success under normal circumstances. As we work to address attendance issues with online school, challenges with student participation, and assignment completion, I grapple with our traditional measures for student success. Daily, I challenge teachers to redefine success in their classrooms and remain open to the possibilities that students may demonstrate learning and growth outside of standardized testing.

I imagine the day when the complete abandonment of testing will lead to results that ensure limitless post-graduate options for students because of a system that refuses to abandon historic protocols for evaluating educational success. Our present reality, however, is that despite numerous attempts, we are still required to administer standardized tests.

Although these tests will not be used against teachers and schools, the sustained expectation to administer tests sustains the narrative that the test is more valuable and important than the well-being of students and staff. How do we reconcile the unfairness of standardized testing (before the pandemic) with the inequities that are associated with testing students and holding ramifications when school, today, is far from the form that was in existence when the testing expectation was first introduced? I am hopeful that the very presence of crisis has introduced dialogue about how we measure student growth in ways that would not have happened without this necessity.

The final and most disheartening reality of all, during my unexpected principalship induction, was the pandemic-magnified disparity between the needs of students and the ability of schools to meet these needs. Each week, I lobbied for more computers, more hot spots, food benefits, housing supports and more to aid our school community members in navigating the tumultuous terrain of life during COVID-19.

As a school leader, I fought against the feeling of defeat as I spoke with district leadership and community partners to try to meet the long list of needs for our school community. After much hard work and deliberation, the return of students was delayed. However, I ended my 16-day run with pride, knowing that I'd left no stone unturned. We were prepared to return.

Although the teachers weren't excited about having me at the helm, no one could deny that my leadership was an asset and not a liability. This experience affirmed for me, my capability and desire to lead a school. As we face reorganization due to enrollment, and my position is in jeopardy, I am excitedly applying for principal positions, thanks to the reassurance provided to me by my first 16 days.

(Since the time this chapter was written, Dr. Coleman has accepted a position as a high school principal.)

Gretchen Bridgers
Teacher Coach and Trainer

Gretchen is a National Board Certified Teacher from Charlotte, NC. In 2006, Gretchen received her bachelor's degree at Marist College in Poughkeepsie, New York. In 2010, she received her master's degree in Curriculum and Supervision from the University of North Carolina at Charlotte.

Gretchen taught grades 2, 3, and 5 before transitioning into the role of a New Teacher Development Coach for The New Teacher Project (TNTP). During this time, she also published her first book for new teachers called "Elementary EDUC 101: What They Didn't Teach You in College" to help prepare future teachers for the realities of life in the classroom.

For more than a decade, Gretchen has passionately mentored and coached educators, lead professional development experiences for school building staff, and presented at district and national conferences. Her impact continues to amplify serving educators worldwide through her blog, podcast, classroom resources, professional development courses and personalized coaching opportunities. Whether you're teaching a lesson or learning one yourself, it's *always a lesson*!

www.alwaysalesson.com

Effectively Developing and Supporting the Growth of Teachers

By Gretchen Bridgers

T eachers have a tremendous impact on generations of children who will lead our future. For that reason, it is imperative that their daily work successfully grows student skill sets in preparation for that future.

Sadly, if teachers enter the profession without adequate or proper training and remain under-supported while on the job, the effect of low teacher performance will negatively impact generations of students. This means those students' skills do not grow to fruition, impacting their performance in their own future jobs. Additionally, 40-50% of teachers who are not supported will leave the profession in five years (Ingersoll and Kralik, 2004), creating a major loss in financial and time investment from the schools who hired and trained them and now have to start over.

If the goal of education is to provide top-notch education to children, then the work begins with supporting the ones leading them in the classroom. That support can take on a variety of roles, but the mission of each role is to support the growth of teachers so that they can support the growth of their students.

My Teacher Support Story

I always dreamed of becoming a teacher. I put on my mom's high heels and taught my stuffed animals in the living room. When I was bored with that approach, I begged my parents to come play along. My mother was a star student, raising her hand and participating often. My father was busy copying my mom's paper, poking her, and shouting out his answers. When I begged him to stop, he would say, "I am just preparing you for what you'll face in the classroom." Boy, was he right!

Every Christmas, Santa brought me supplies for my future classroom. I read books about teaching, started a pen and sticker collection, and later turned the garage into a classroom with an oversized world map covering the wall. My feet were planted firmly in my future.

When I landed my first teaching job, my natural talent had others convinced that I didn't need help. I hosted a student teacher in my third year while, ironically, still being a member of the new teacher mentorship program in the district. Although I appreciated that my principal left me alone to figure out my style of teaching, my potential started to wane.

My assigned mentor taught a different grade level and her classroom was in a different hallway than mine. Our schedules rarely matched up and when we did meet, it was to check off and sign a monthly meeting document. I ended up taking all my urgent questions to my team of colleagues, which I realize was unfair as they didn't sign up to spend time helping me grow. Someone else was getting a mentorship stipend to "help" me, yet their "help" wasn't working.

Luckily, I figured out a lot on my own. I had been preparing myself for this role since I was young, and I was very resourceful in finding what I needed when I needed it. I survived. Sadly, it took three times as long to be as effective as I could have been had I had proper guidance and support from the beginning.

As I gained experience hosting student teachers, mentoring new staff members in the building, leading my grade level team, along with providing professional development (PD) to school and district teachers, I realized I had a new teaching passion. By teaching teachers, I had the opportunity to give back in the best way I knew how- being the support I wish I had had as a teacher.

I originally left the classroom to coach new teachers in kindergarten through 12th grade in my large, urban school district. Watching teacher performance skyrocket over a three-month intensive cohort model followed by individualized on-the-job coaching taught me what I always knew. When you offer personalized, ongoing support, you see massive growth results.

This led me to create my own educational business, Always A Lesson, that supports the growth and development of teachers through PD courses as well as mentorship and coaching services. I wanted to ensure no one's teaching potential would stagnate as mine did. I would be there personally to help them on an ongoing basis that helping their talent unfold in record time. This has been my greatest accomplishment- becoming the teacher leader I so desperately needed and wanted for myself.

The Implementation of Teacher Support Models

Teacher support refers to any strategy, tool or opportunity that aims to increase the knowledge and skill of a teacher. The purpose of teacher support models is to grow the capacity of teacher performance that results in academic growth for students in the classroom.

Even with recent positive changes to teacher support models, a continuous revision is still necessary for creating teacher proficiency growth and development over time. Employing a responsive, flexible model ensures as the educational landscape changes, so does the teacher support model. Using outdated methods on new, current problems is why so many teachers are facing burnout, lack of job satisfaction and plateaued skillsets. All of this has a negative impact on student learning.

Models of Teacher Support

The following models are critical components to support the development and growth of teachers. They range from light to intensive support and focus on strengthening different teacher skills. By implementing a growth continuum for teachers of varying proficiency levels, ongoing and personalized support will ensure success for all.

New Hire Onboarding

When a teacher joins a staff for the first time, there's a process to support their assimilation into the school climate and culture. This process includes reviewing items such as mission and vision statements, policies, school year calendar, staff directory, site map, building access information, drill procedures, required duties, grade level schedules and more. This level of support is responsive and individualized.

Recommendation: Every school needs to create and provide a thorough onboarding experience to eliminate common pitfalls for new hires. Putting time in up front to lay the groundwork and frontload common questions they have ensures success in the long run. However, there is a difference between new hire onboarding and staff orientation. Onboarding is acclimating to the learning environment. Orientation is acclimating to the building.

Many schools provide the orientation but few onboard their staff. When this step is missing, teacher growth stagnates. It is as if they have to hunt down each puzzle piece and put all of them together by themselves instead of receiving the puzzle pieces altogether.

Onboarding eliminates the guesswork and lessens the struggle. It is efficient and effective for getting new hires on track confidently. Strong onboarding processes appoint a teacher leader to run the experience. These leaders pull together important documents as a reference packet, design an agenda, and block off time and space to complete the onboarding process. This is beneficial for two reasons. First, it provides authentic leadership opportunities for teachers. Second, the experience of onboarding with peers fosters immediate collaboration.

Lastly, the onboarding process should be specific to the needs of the new hire. By creating "onboarding tracks," the experience may be tailored to the new hire. This means whether they are a beginning teacher out of college, a beginning teacher via an alternate certification program with life and other career experiences, a veteran out-of-state or district teacher, or an internal transfer candidate, they receive relevant, appropriate onboarding experiences. Each of these new hires differ in the type of onboarding support needed to help them begin effortlessly and successfully.

Peer Mentorship

Once on the job, new teachers in years 0-3 are paired with an expert colleague so they can meet together monthly to answer any questions, share lesson ideas, and problem-solve to address varied obstacles. Colleagues also come together in professional learning communities (PLCs) to plan effective lessons, devise strategies to meet a range of learners and analyze data points. Peer mentorship is a moderate level of teacher support varying in personalization depending on the consistency of the methods and investment of peer support members.

Recommendation: An informal ongoing mentorship model for teachers 0-3 would eliminate compliance-based meetings to sign off on mentorship paperwork. Having a mentorship meeting checklist is helpful in providing a focus for each meeting, but mentors should be offering frequent assistance beyond Q/A – observations, co-planning, co-teaching, data digs, etc.

PLCs are an opportunity for colleagues to collaborate and lead their own learning. Protocols, norms, agendas, and facilitated conversations with a coach can replace old habits of silent, solo lesson planning. Peer colleagues also have the opportunity to learn from each other through Learning

Walks—a process where teachers observe each other teaching live in front of students to gather ideas to better their craft. No official mentorship title is required, just showcasing great teaching among staff.

These three peer mentorship options accelerate teacher proficiency growth, regardless of their level of experience.

Individualized Coaching

A specialist or instructional coach is hired to work with teachers one-on-one, small group or staff wide. They are often content area experts helping implement curriculum with fidelity but can also be high quality instructional leaders who focus on data, technology or the planning and delivery of lessons. This type of teacher support is the most intensive and personalized to the unique needs of teachers.

Recommendation: In addition to providing PD and being a resource when needed, instructional coaches should use coaching cycles to provide specific support to teachers based on their needs and current level of performance. A coaching cycle includes pre-observation, observation, and post-observation debriefing. Although this is similar to administrative walk-throughs, any data collected is not recorded formally. Instead, the information gleaned is solely to improve performance.

During these cycles, coaches look at student data to help teachers plan differentiated instruction, practice upcoming lesson delivery, provide bite-sized feedback on instructional strategies, and aid in the reflective habit-building of teachers. This way, they know what to work on, why it is important, and how they should improve their craft. By using a structured approach for supporting the growth and development of teachers, coaching work becomes more intentional and strategic, which results in increased teacher proficiency and student achievement.

Virtual Components

As schools transitioned to online environments due to the Covid-19 pandemic, teacher supports were transferred virtually as well. The reality is that virtual components are going to be the norm, post-pandemic. This means we have another aspect of teacher support that we have to get right to reach the impact we desire. The question many leaders haven't figured out yet is, "How do we hold teachers accountable in a virtual environment?"

Recommendation: The pandemic has created a unique opportunity for teacher growth. Educators had to get creative and innovative under intense time constraints and without clear guidance or training. Formal evaluations were put on the back burner and all staff members rolled up their sleeves to help no matter what their title.

This perfect storm of an opportunity allowed teachers to take risks in the classroom, try out new technology tools, and use a variety of engagement strategies more than ever before. Although it has been a tumultuous, challenging time, teacher proficiency has increased for those I personally supported. This unforeseen circumstance created an environment conducive for productive failure—a low-risk environment to get better faster.

This should become the standard environment in all teacher support models. For example, more opportunities for teachers to take charge of lesson design and delivery, explore various teaching methods and tools, and teach creatively without penalty. Virtual components like student discussion boards, short learning videos, and Q/A office hours increased student achievement and engagement, as stated by teachers. These components should be built into in-person learning environments as a continuation of the learning day and be how we hold teachers accountable for strong instruction. By supporting students like we support teachers (on an ongoing basis and in a variety of ways), they will become just as successful.

Next Steps

To better support teachers, develop strategies that are flexible in responding to teacher needs and wants while also building in models that have stood the test of time. Your recommended next steps are to *Review, Revise & Refresh* your teacher support plan.

- Review all current offerings,

- Revise offerings that are outdated and/or not working, and

- Refresh the plan with new offerings that are responsive and personalized.

The goal of any type of teacher support plan you create is to provide guidance on an ongoing basis. It does not always have to be a large-scale, intensive opportunity. Sometimes, the quick informal check-ins on teacher well-being carry the biggest impact. Keep showing up for them and they will keep showing up for you.

As a reminder, student achievement is the byproduct of teacher efficacy. Developing and supporting the growth of teachers so that they are more effective in the classroom has a domino effect that trickles down to the success of students. Students cannot perform at high levels if those that lead them in the classroom are not well-trained and coached to be their best. Ultimately, if we do not care for the root of the problem, we will never see the fruit on the vine. When we prioritize the growth and development of teachers, we will reap the reward of student achievement for generations to come!

References

- Ingersoll, R., & Kralik, J. (2004). The Impact of Mentoring on Teacher Retention: What the Research Says. Denver, CO: The Education Commission of the States.

Giuliana Conti
Music Teacher – Doctoral Candidate

Giuliana Conti is a Ph.D. candidate at the University of Washington studying the intersections of music education, ethnomusicology, and social justice. She graduated from UC Berkeley with her BA in music and then taught world music education at the elementary level for five years before returning to school herself to pursue her MA and now Ph.D. She has taught in over five countries and believes it is important for all education professionals to consider music as a core subject and incorporate it into daily education, with cultural diversity and critical race theory at the core of instruction. She researches intercultural competence development through exposure to diverse musical experiences, and is currently completing her dissertation on the knowledge, development, and programming choices of freeform Radio DJs. She has additional experience in lobbying, student leadership, and higher education. She is a lucky cat mom and daughter of two amazing parents.

Instagram: @Grad_gal.

The Need for Music throughout our Post-COVID Education Ecosystem

By Giuliana Conti

When you visualize music education, what does it look like to you? Think about who the teacher is, what type of music you imagine being taught, and how the students are interacting together in the classroom. Where did this impression of music education come from? And if you experienced it personally, was it enjoyable? I am always interested in people's perceptions of school music because, in my experience as a researcher, it so often represents the very issues our discipline has been working hard to dismantle. Stereotypically, this usually includes assumptions about mandatory instrumental proficiency regardless of student choice, teachers who are unrelatable and dictate but don't listen, as well as a curriculum based entirely on music notation without content that interests the students or activities that extend beyond Western-based ensembles. Music is, of course, so much more than the symphony, band, and choir, but how will kids know this if they do not experience anything outside the norm?

Interestingly, at the onset of conversations about music education, the same people who share disappointing experiences like these also tout, irrefutably, that music must remain in schools and be promoted to the same daily attention given to other core subjects. Somehow, despite feeling irrelevant to many people's lives outside of school, music teaching and learning of any kind continues to leave such an impression that there exists a mutual understanding about its importance throughout child development and into college-age life.

In this chapter, I will unpack why music is an even more important subject to provide across all K-12 curricula post-COVID, and how each member of the education ecosystem can take part in the healing and transformation of our students through music. I will share why this matters to me according to my own life experiences, and why post-COVID is the best opportunity for us to make drastic changes across the education spectrum, which must include a more culturally diverse music curriculum and broader availability of music learning. I will conclude this chapter with concrete calls to action and ideas for the next steps.

Our Challenge

Countless research exists which correlates music learning with heightened learning capabilities in other subjects, increased socioemotional development, and the development of competencies necessary to interact with unknown people and ideas. Yet, even with the promotion of music to the status of a core subject in the Obama Administration's Every Student Succeeds Act, music and other arts subjects continue to face growth obstacles. (1)

Researchers and practitioners in music education rely on momentum to propel the discipline forward, which comes in large part from our own community, but also from increased engagement with education professionals outside of music education. The landscape of music education is and has been drastically changing toward a more inclusive and diverse practice, but we have faced considerable challenges in building adequate momentum toward these goals, largely in part to an overall misunderstanding by other educators and policy makers about what music education is and where we want it to go.

We want students to see themselves in the curriculum and feel motivated to continue with music beyond K-12. Students who are able to connect more deeply with the music education they experience are thereby more likely to remain thoughtful music consumers as they age, who then continue to support the music industry, and maybe play an instrument throughout their lifetime as a hobby or in a more serious capacity.

The goal of music education is not to carve out technically proficient musical robots through blood, sweat, and tears. Music is a global phenomenon deeply entrenched in local and international communities and represents the intersectionality of the human experience. (2) When we play or listen to music, we are activating more neural pathways in the brain than any other subject or activity we can engage in. (3)

It is no wonder that millions of people around the world connect with music personally, emotionally, culturally, socially, and psychologically. It stands to reason then, that the objective of music education should be to foster a love of music and to teach about the various ways in which music is produced and consumed around the world so that music can be a resource for students through the myriad of capacities it can fulfill. Many educators and researchers understand that through direct engagement and experience with various genres and cultures of music, students can shape their own world. They can apply music throughout their life according to their needs and wants, as we already do with math, writing, and social studies. This is not only happening now in music classrooms across the country, but it is also necessary to include throughout other K-12 classrooms and subjects. Music deserves a more holistic implementation so that messaging about music is more consistent with its existence outside our schools.

My Story

I am a music education researcher and former elementary music teacher of five years. I believe music saved my life. I have made it my mission to work toward an equitable music education which can provide others the same support I experienced, plus more. As a result, I am in the last year of my Ph.D. program and have spent the better part of my life learning about the interaction between music, the brain, the mind, and society. I have barely touched the surface of understanding in a discipline that spans centuries, cultures, and geographic locations. Nevertheless, given my lived experiences and that of those who share similar stories, I am dedicated to the effort of even one student whose life becomes positively changed by music education.

My own relationship with music began as a little girl. Both of my parents were born outside the U.S. and have very worldly tastes in music listening. My father was a talented classical guitarist turned blues, country, and rock musician. I have annoying, but fond memories of him opening all our doors and windows in summer to blast riffs on his electric guitar. He had the amp turned up to ten, at which point my mom and I would share one look of horror and rush out to get ice cream. We used any excuse to save our eardrums. Whether it was my dad singing and playing music, the radio, or CDs and cassettes, music was always on in our house.

When I was about six or seven, my mom became chronically ill and both of my parents lost their business. A few years later, my dad developed liver failure, which left him almost incapacitated for about five years. Shortly after his diagnosis, when I was eleven, we lost everything in our house to toxic mold, a year after which we needed to move cities for my dad's transplant (which he did receive).

To say I lost everything I knew is an understatement. I didn't recognize my surroundings and, in many cases, even my parents for a good ten years. The social isolation was debilitating and I was frequently failing classes. To be honest, I remember very little from when I was eight to sixteen and have been formally diagnosed with PTSD, which continues to affect my everyday life.

This is important to my overall point because I often imagine how long it will take for me to heal and make sense of these traumas throughout my life. Yet, even with these traumas, my privilege as a white middle-class child prevented me from experiencing further layers of racism and bigotry and subjected to so many students who may spend their entire life navigating a broken system of oppression.

My adversity is a glimpse into that which many of my students continue to be subjected to on top of any unpredictable traumas like my own. This is part of what drives me and why I am calling on you to reflect throughout this chapter.

As I have developed over the past few decades, I have come to recognize that music listening was the one equilibrium and source of therapy I had at my disposal during these years of trauma, and which I attribute to saving my life. I believe I am not alone when I share that there were moments of temptation in my environment that would have allowed me to escape through drug use and inappropriate behavior. For me, all of this would have likely led to a future I prefer not to think about. The desire for escapism and was strong, and I feel so fortunate to have found restorative effects by listening to my music, alone, in my room.

But this was a learned behavior, music listening for emotional well-being was modeled to me at home. I spent years watching my mom suffer with yet unexplained illnesses that left her often bedridden in the dark. (It later made more sense when we realized the walls, floors, and ceilings were almost entirely taken over by black mold beneath the paint and carpet). So in those moments of despair when she could no longer make sense of her own life, my dad would carry the two-foot-tall stereo speakers into their bedroom and curate playlists of the most excruciating opera.

My father is from Rome and has a deep familiarity with Italian opera, a love my mom adopted throughout their relationship and trickled down to me. I will never forget seeing the door close behind him and hearing the painful cries of singer Maria Callas drowning out the tormented sobs of my own mom, my favorite person, on the other side of the wall. It was then that I made sense of what music was for, and without knowing it, I became purposeful in my choice of music for my own emotional regulation and well-being.

It was when I found my dad's Bob Marley collection that my life really changed. By the time I was six, I had memorized every word to four of his albums. I was curating my own recorded cassette tapes and essentially building emotionally categorized song lists for my various needs. As I got more comfortable and familiar with the other music in our 200+ CD collection, music in other languages and from cultures began to feel normal.

I would crave new sounds, grabbing any CD I could get my hands on. By the age of ten, I was mixing CDs with artists like the Gypsy Kings, Karumanta Jamuyku, John Lee Hooker, Louis Prima, Chet Baker, and Strunz & Farah, all based on similarities around how the music made me feel.

Thinking about my professional trajectory, it has been the healing and belonging I found in music to which I have dedicated myself. By understanding the underlying mechanisms which drove my listening habits, I can then support the inclusion of these elements into everyday education - for the benefit of students' wellbeing.

Children deserve the agency and access to develop these skills themselves, and there is no reason why music education has to be relegated to once a week, or that it must be limited to instrumental learning and Western Classical music. Interestingly, my own school music, which started with classical viola in 4th grade, was so contradictory to my personal music interests and listening habits, eventually to the point where after a degree in music performance, I almost entirely quit.

I needed time to reconsider what being a musician meant in my life. Did I ever really want it? Or was it the closest option I had to any musical engagement through what my school had to offer? There was no music listening or discussions in my classrooms, only music notation and orchestra. And if I did not identify with the Western classical music we played, despite being raised with a fair amount of exposure to it, thanks to my dad, I can't imagine how my classmates felt about the same program.

Considering the diversity of our national student population, children deserve an exposure to music and other forms of human expression, which better represents their own community and personal identity. These changes are happening slowly within the world of music education but given the drastic changes to our education system in the past year, we have an incredible opportunity post-pandemic to include music in everyday learning. Students and teachers may benefit from the many outcomes which take place when listening to, interacting with, and playing music they can relate to.

Why Post-COVID Matters

When No Child Left Behind transitioned to the Every Student Succeeds Act during the Obama administration (4), Music and several other academic subjects were elevated to the core curriculum, which was previously isolated to math, science, history, and language arts. These four main academic core subjects have been prioritized over the past fifty years.

This is, in part, due to the mid-20th-century space race, which demanded working class citizens develop the necessary skills to contribute to the scientific advancement of the U.S. The effects of this emphasis led to multiple generations of K-12 curriculum, designed primarily for assessment measurability and college readiness. (5)

Unfortunately, one of the side-effects of this multi-decade emphasis on few isolated subjects has been the inconsistent implementation and availability of other subjects like music, art, dance, physical education, social studies, and those with less tangible and measurable learning outcomes. (6)

Due to stronger assessment-based priorities in schools, a common stereotype in education now is that music and art programs are first to be cut in the face of budget shortages. (7) Ironically, however, there seems to exist a widely understood positive correlation between music--as well as other arts subjects--and student academic success.

Countless books and articles have been published on the topic of heightened learning in math, history, and language arts alongside music learning. (8) Yet, the inconsistency of arts education remains more consistent than its availability across K-12 grades, especially where socioeconomic status affects a school or district's budget. Music teachers and arts advocates have felt like they are screaming into a void about the importance of these subjects in schools, despite the somehow common understanding that students deserve access to the arts and that the arts are important to a holistic education.

Of course, providing access to the arts is not the only challenge schools face. Our public school system has and may always be confronted with unresolved obstructions like inequitable school funding, racism, outdated curricular materials, and the school to prison pipeline, all of which need to be addressed.

Unfortunately, the ability for education professionals and community members to coordinate and make significant progress for any one topic has felt daunting, and at times futile without the opportunity to build momentum. Improving music education has been an upward battle, for the people who fight tirelessly for change and growth in our education system.

But then 2020 hit and now we face a post-COVID learning environment with more questions than answers. Not only were all school personnel required to change how education is structured, but to develop an increased awareness of the suffering and oppression upon Black, Indigenous, and Brown people. Emphasis was placed on how these and other marginalized populations across the life of this country have suffered multiple layers of grief, processing, action, restructuring, and contemplation on everyone's part.

All members of the educational ecosystem--parents, kids, staff, teachers, administrators, legislators, and community members--were suddenly thrown into a live-work condition so unknown. For many, it created a shared experience of emotional awareness and sensitivity. Taking time to watch and engage in what was happening in our country transitioned into facing something we were all forced to watch 24-7 from our living room confinement.

Teaching is an already emotionally laborious profession, and now anyone connected to education could see the cataclysmic effects of current events on the well-being of our student population and teaching force. Suddenly, the media became the most prominent part of our lives, more than the already unusual amount, and everyone watched as the dark realities of our country coated every aspect of life like the ash that blanketed our eastern states days after 9/11.

I want to be clear. The patterns of racism and abuse I am referring to from the past year, of which many people have become suddenly aware, existed long before 2020. Mass shootings and murdered Black people are not new phenomena in the U.S.; and neither are illness, death, and a poorly structured healthcare system. It is undeniable, however, that the isolation of COVID, the emotional turmoil of COVID losses so closely related to much of our population, the plummeted job market, obscene unemployment levels, as well as fear of the unknown, exacerbated the experience we all shared as members of this society.

So looking ahead we were all trying to get all students back on track. But is that really the goal? Or, now that we have been forced to experience every part of living in a different capacity, can we exploit the opportunity we now have to take this weird, blended, and fragmented system of education and redesign it in a way that honors the change so many have been screaming for? The building blocks of education are all jumbled and disorganized anyway. Why not use them to rebuild something more structurally sound?

Now, and finally, with this renewed opportunity ahead of us, we can implement a more consistent and fulfilling curriculum with music education, arts education, physical education, and other necessary subjects rightfully alongside the other main core subjects.

Education is an ecosystem, so in order for music to become a strong part of the healing process for students, as well as their socio-emotional development post-covid, all stakeholders will need to consider their role in supporting educational advancement over the next few years. Music matters, and now the education community can benefit from the richness that comes with a music education when everyone is supportive and involved. So long as we all play our part.

The Directives

Music educators: Now more than ever, we must think about the content of our curricula and the way students engage with music in our classrooms. General elementary music educators have the strongest ability to diversify the cultures and origins of the music they choose to bring to their students because the nature of their discipline is more exploratory and open-ended. They also have, perhaps, the greatest responsibility given the levels of psychological and sociological development children experience between the ages of 4-10.

By learning necessary online research skills and the importance of culturally responsive pedagogy, general elementary teachers can and should attempt to build programs that include student input and interest, music from international languages and cultures, and different ways of experiencing music through dance, singing, performance, discussion, and investigation, as closely related to the culture of origin as possible.

Students have been stuck inside for a year and may not know how to vocalize how they feel coming back into the classroom, so play will be incredibly important to their health and well-being. Furthermore, using music to promote discussions about feelings, in general, can help provide different ways of communicating how they feel and outlets for at home.

For music educators who are responsible for ensemble-based teaching, encouraging students to choose their instruments as well as provide input toward what music the ensemble learns. This will likely lead to higher levels of investment and satisfaction for everyone involved.

While there tends to be less time for discussion or different ways of experiencing music in an ensemble (for example, through dance), students can still develop listening, research, arrangement, and composition skills. Then they can apply them to styles of music they are more passionate about.

Encourage students to see instruments as a tool they can use for any style of music and for any purpose they need throughout their lifespan. Limiting the styles and cultures of music they play on their instruments can easily become the same as simply providing them the fish to eat, per the old proverb. Instead, teach them to fish by providing diverse musical skill sets and experiences they can build on for years to come. And no matter what grade or subject you teach, reach out to music education organizations which are already supporting these efforts and be patient with the process as it is meant to be communal, not isolating.

General educators: Whatever subject you teach, music belongs. If you teach other languages, include music in those languages. If you discuss history or social studies, music can show students how a time period sounded and what type of topics were important at that time. Music can help facilitate conversations about race, oppression, and adversity without having to directly speak about issues they may not fully understand.

If you struggle with behavioral challenges or lack of classroom social cohesion, there are resources to help you learn how music can build community and calm students. The idea is more about living through your day-to-day teaching experiences with an eye toward healing and community building, knowing that music and the arts are a resource for you and your class.

You do not need to be musically trained to include music in your classroom. And while the fear of misrepresenting another person's culture is real, your training in pedagogy is enough to help you succeed. It is better to try than to do nothing at all.

What is important post-COVID is that students experience school subjects through multiple mediums given the lonely online year of education they have had to endure. Music can make curricular milestones fun and engaging and provide creative or emotional outlets to students who might otherwise not have opportunities to build these skills themselves.

A few ideas that can work from kindergarten through high school includes rewriting song lyrics and using karaoke videos on YouTube to learn a new subject. Students can share their favorite music in class as an ice breaker at the beginning of the year, and then you can play the collection of songs in the background of class throughout the year to help students feel grounded and validated in their own interests.

Students can also learn beat making software which they can use together as a class to coordinate a performance about an important historical event, or subject, similar to the idea of *Hamilton* the musical or other genres the students are interested in. Overall, music exists for these students in many, many forms dissimilar to how it is traditionally taught in school.

So now that they have experienced a year of discomfort and isolation, how can you use music to build up your students while also messaging through its inclusion in your classroom that it is a regular part of life which deserves regular attention?

Parents: You know your children best. Are they okay? How have they and you experienced this past year as a family as well as individuals? Music can be a wonderful tool at home for connection and fun. Is there music your kids listen to which you can become more involved with? Are there concerts coming up which you can plan for as a family? Is there an artist or style of music that is or used to be prominent in your household which can be used to make space for family storytelling and nostalgia?

Using music during activities like cooking, getting ready for school in the morning, or winding down for sleep at the end of the day can foster healing energy, build lasting memories, and help children learn how to use music as an active element in their lives.

Music can also be a way to meet other community members and better understand current events, which may be difficult for children to understand or talk about. Like my story, we cannot always know what our younger generation is really grappling with as they may not have fully developed the ability to reflect, process, and communicate what is in their minds and hearts.

Music is a powerful tool we can provide for them to learn to regulate themselves and build a strong sense of self. The more you can integrate music as a family and encourage their own relationship with music, the stronger your child may become as they grow and develop as an individual.

Administrators: You are a crucial gatekeeper for the inclusion of music across schools and disciplines. If you are in a position of authority and affect change in any way in your school, district, or state, the open support and encouragement for cross-disciplinary music engagement can make the difference for students who may not otherwise have access to the arts or other mental health and wellbeing resources. Culturally diverse music in our classrooms sends the message that the identity of our diverse students matters, as do the communities which exist outside our classrooms.

Teachers also deserve support as they reintegrate into classrooms and hopefully try new ways of teaching and learning with their students to offset the past year of isolation and remote education. Your push for skill development in music and the arts can increase the likelihood of student success and overall positive school experiences.

Here are helpful resources for anyone trying to elevate music in their school and life:

- Smithsonian Folkways
- NAfME National Association for Music Education

- Local teachers' unions
- KEXP.org
- Local and global non-profit music organizations
- Routledge World Music Pedagogy Book Series

Music integration is one step and one option, but one which represents messaging and prioritization that can span generations of change if you take the opportunity now to rethink how our education system is currently functioning, and how we can be creative during the healing process post-COVID to make lasting change through the arts.

References

- See works by Patricia Shehan Campbell, Carlos Abril, Constance McKoy, and Kathryn Marsh
- Parncutt, Richard, and Gary McPherson, eds. The science and psychology of music performance: Creative strategies for teaching and learning. Oxford University Press, 2002.
- https://www.ed.gov/essa?src=ft
- Ezrati, Milton. "Our Dangerous Obsession With STEM." Academic Questions 33 (2020): 307-313.
- Eric E. Branscome (2012) The Impact of Education Reform on Music Education: Paradigm Shifts in Music Education Curriculum, Advocacy, and Philosophy from Sputnik to Race to the Top, Arts Education Policy Review, 113:3, 112-118, DOI: 10.1080/10632913.2012.687341
- Lauren Kapalka Richerme (2012) Remain or React: The Music Education Profession's Responses to Sputnik and A Nation at Risk, Arts Education Policy Review, 113:1, 35-44, DOI: 10.1080/10632913.2012.626385
- José Luis Aróstegui (2016) Exploring the global decline of music education, Arts Education Policy Review, 117:2, 96-103, DOI: 10.1080/10632913.2015.1007406
- Holochwost, S. J., Propper, C. B., Wolf, D. P., Willoughby, M. T., Fisher, K. R., Kolacz, J., Volpe, V. V., & Jaffee, S. R. (2017). Music education, academic achievement, and executive functions. Psychology of Aesthetics, Creativity, and the Arts, 11(2), 147–166. https://doi.org/10.1037/aca0000112

Dr. Joy Acaso
Anxiety Support Coach and Family Therapist

Joy is a wife and mom of two: a 13-year-old daughter and seven-year-old son. She and her husband enjoy nature and taking ther children to the beach or biking trails. They encourage parents to intentionally build their family toolbox of emotional resilience so they can raise children who are confident in their self-worth.

Joy values the integrity and uniqueness of everyone she meets. She puts awe and curiosity at the forefront because she knows that "one-size-fits-all" can never bring healing. She has made it her mission to spread awareness in utilizing therapy and coaching as a means of helping families bond closer and make their mental health their priority.

Joy provides resources for individuals and families dealing with chronic anxiety. Her practice offers various levels of support such as workshops, free guides, online courses, group coaching and 1:1 coaching.

www.joyacaso.com

Mental Wellness for Teachers and Students

By Joy Acaso

S tress is silent and, over time, can become deadly. However, when we speak of students, stress isn't really all that silent. In fact, one can easily tell when a teenager isn't feeling so well. They start to act out. As these emotions show up, students are reprimanded and teachers are inundated with more tasks than they ever asked for in the first place. But this has always been the state of American education and we as a society have gotten used to it. Here we are always discussing, wishing and hoping that we can raise the next generation of responsible adults.

Can we visualize what responsible adults do? Our culture focuses highly on outcomes and productivity that we are most likely racing robots. What if we were more proactive as a culture rather than reactive? What would responsible adults look like and what would they be doing? We throw in words such as confident, accountable and caring as well. But these characteristics are not automatic. They go against the grain of our very flesh. Human development studies show us that babies begin with the understanding that their world is the only world that exists. We call this the egocentric stage.

At the age of four, children begin to make sense of having a world outside of their own. Empathy at this point doesn't just kick in. Someone other than themselves needs to show them what empathy looks like. What tends to happen is a separation is created. If you observe children in their natural habitat, you can see that they live without inhibitions. They are decisive. How do we know this? They tell their parents what they want unapologetically. Children also ask tons of questions. Their perspective is first borne out of curiosity. Until an adult steps in, there is no separation.

When responsibility, accountability and self-confidence enter the picture, we seem to draw a line. As if being unapologetic means the opposite. Or that curiosity is no longer valid. Inside our classrooms and our own homes, we forget the student in front of us. We easily pick up on the task that they need to finish. We check off every item on their to-do list and ours. Was this ever the right thing to do?

Last year alone, the emergency room was filled with students and teens walking in for having experienced panic attacks. The social isolation has turned them inwards with nothing to console them. They haven't been given ample guidance on how to build that inner strength. Now Tik-Tok has become their new textbook. They have started diagnosing themselves as they take those five-point questionnaires.

These students are coming home and telling their parents that they have anxiety. Can you guess the response they receive? They're told, "no, you don't," without being heard. Dialogues are very often absent in schools and among families. We jump to conclusions with little to no evidence. And yet, students are being accused right and left of catastrophizing their situations.

Who was supposed to show them how to stop the chaos from escalating? They're busy with Algebra, Biology and end-of-year exams. Those are great and have always been essential towards learning. We have, unfortunately, assigned them to be a catchall for what looks like growth and responsibility. They're moving right along the milestones and guidelines. Emotionally, and socially they are regressing.

By giving students and their families access to resources on social and emotional learning (SEL), we are essentially prioritizing their mental wellness. Teachers benefit tremendously as well. Under the umbrella of SEL, we can bring in mindfulness. This approach will then lead to building a skill set for combatting stress.

If we want students who are able to exercise self-control, cooperation and positive communication, we can leverage SEL. Along with mindfulness, teachers and students can bridge the gap between being constantly pulled to produce and perform and the need to be mentally well in the midst of all of it.

A curriculum on social and emotional learning can show students practical ways to handle stressful situations. Rather than being hard on themselves or displacing their frustrations on someone else, in time, they can take steps to express their needs. When students act out, it comes from a place of unconscious and impulsive choices. These are habitual reactions that can be replaced.

Students can learn that they don't always have to act on their urges. For example, if they don't understand the instructions for their project, they may feel overwhelmed. They may have the urge to give up. In the process of SEL, they can gain different techniques rather than just giving up.

Mindfulness can also serve as a healthier approach to their emotions and negative thoughts. Their feelings can be read as data instead of something that needs to be fixed. A couple of months ago, my seven-year-old son was going through a stressful time that manifested as a tantrum. He kept saying that he didn't want to go to school that day. Had I not sat down with him patiently, I wouldn't have known that a simple activity was at the root of the matter. Every Monday, they are required to write about their weekend.

During the pandemic, we were doing much of the same things. It turned out my son needed help with the details of his writing. The tantrum was a cry for help. I stayed with him that morning, having the conversation and teaching him to let the energy move through his body. These aren't innate to humans. We want to protect ourselves.

A child's brain is no different. They fear doing hard things. Uncertainty doesn't bring comfort. When these big feelings come up, if they haven't been taught or modeled what words to say, they will find an outlet. It can be healthy or unhealthy but an outlet nonetheless.

Once a 17-year-old told me that one of her fears was becoming an adult. I could have come up with many assumptions as to why one would be afraid. The younger generation these days are more forthcoming. When the timing is right and there is mutual trust, they speak their mind. She then told me that "Adults are boring. They don't listen to music. They stop taking vacations." This is the example they see. It leaves an imprint in their mind that there's no stopping in between. One must keep working hard. Is this truly the message we want them to remember?

Mindfulness is the antidote against irrational fears. It is built on the principles of awe, curiosity and acceptance among others. These take the place of criticism and judgment. The result then are teachers and parents who take the time to work with their students rather than fixing their emotions. Students are more likely to seek help and engage in discussions in this kind of environment. Social and emotional learning and mindfulness are built on the premise that all feelings are valid. All thoughts, negative and positive, are also valid. This is the essence of our humanity.

Having emotions is not a disorder. We all experience anxiety. Students are frantic because these feelings have been labeled, "bad." Scientifically, all feelings are neutral. They are neither good nor bad. Mindfulness reinforces this too. Teachers and students can take the cue from mindfulness techniques that "all feelings are welcome here."

When students (and their teachers) aren't overthinking about how others would judge them if they mention how angry, frustrated or sad they are, then they can focus on what matters. It is important they explore healthy ways of coping with their circumstances.

With the methods under SEL, students can engage in conversations about self-awareness. Teachers can ask what makes them anxious. What do they usually do when they're sad? Students can share within a group where it is safe to talk about feelings. They can learn from their teachers and each other. In addition, SEL can increase their self-confidence.

Both students and teachers can discuss strategies that work for them and strategies that work. As the facilitator, the teacher can offer suggestions for students to try and apply in their own situations. They can take activities with them as well to try at home with their families. Not only will they be able to practice, they will see results and progress.

SEL and mindfulness can be integrated as a stand-alone program. Schools can offer them as elective or an extracurricular activity. Another option could be for teachers to incorporate bite-sized lessons in their existing plans. Students will learn to observe their own thoughts before their stress escalates. This will encourage positive mindset and behaviors in the classroom and beyond.

Dr. Monica Batiste
Associate Superintendent

Dr. Monica Batiste currently serves as the associate superintendent for Human Resources and Talent Management of Gwinnett County Public Schools, the 13th largest school district in the nation, with 180,000 students and more than 12,500 teaching staff. Dr. Batiste's responsibilities include supervising the preparation and administration of human resource allotments, the recruitment, screening, referral, and placement of staff for employment, and the processing and maintenance of all applicant records. She also directs the establishment and maintenance of a comprehensive and value-added benefits and leave administration system, the program for wage and salary administration, and the preparation of the monthly personnel recommendations for the CEO/Superintendent of Schools.

Dr. Batiste has previously served as a teacher, principal, assistant principal, and district office executive director. During her 30 years in education, she has earned a reputation for developing and nurturing district leaders, local school leaders, teachers, and students through a commitment to mentoring and coaching, focusing on teaching and learning.

Dr. Batiste is an alumnus of Mercer University in Atlanta, Georgia. She attended graduate school at Brenau University and McNeese State University.

Instagram: @BatisteMonica

Keysha Robinson
Director of Special Education Staffing

Educator and leader in the Gwinnett County School District, Keysha Robinson, started her career as a special education teacher and department chair after receiving her Bachelor's Degree in Learning Disabilities from Mercer University. Later, she earned a Master's Degree in Educational Leadership and an Educational Specialist in Curriculum and Instruction. After teaching, she became a district leader as a Special Education Coordinator and then served as Director of Special Education Compliance. Currently, she is the Director of Special Education Staffing in Human Resources and Talent Management.

Her experiences as an educator and district leader helped shape her understanding of the importance of having prepared educators in every classroom to ensure equity and quality instruction for all students. Thus, she designed the Special Education Internship Program to recruit and retain university graduates to serve students with disabilities. The program has been successful as it is an innovative approach to teacher preparation which provides a realistic job preview, relevant professional learning, and ongoing mentorship. This layered approach to teacher preparation increases teacher confidence, yielding better student outcomes and increasing retention of new special educators.

Keysha believes her greatest accomplishment is her teenage son. She and her son enjoy sports activities, traveling, and spending time with family and friends.

Keysha.robinson@gcpsk12.org

Teacher Shortage

By Dr. Monica Batiste and Keysha Robinson

T he current teacher shortage continues to persist and challenges school districts to look for new and innovative ways to attract and retain teachers. The teacher shortage has become more complicated as schools focus on specific subgroups such as special education, second language learners, math and science, students of color, and students from low-socioeconomic backgrounds.

The need for school districts to secure quality teachers to influence positive student outcomes in these areas increases annually due to the challenges associated with these dynamic factors. School districts also struggle to retain special education teachers due to low pay and subpar teacher preparation.

Dr. Sid Camp, Executive Director of Human Resources and Talent Management with Gwinnett County Public Schools, the largest school system in Georgia and 14th largest in the nation, confirms this notion, "Over the past thirty years, recruiting and retaining special education teachers has been a challenge." Dr. Camp has worked in several school districts in Georgia and recollects the same special education recruitment and retention challenges that he has served as a Human Resources professional.

Consequently, schools serving the most vulnerable population see several teachers leaving the profession within three to five years. In addition, many of these teachers are challenged with meeting the Individuals with Disabilities Act (IDEA) and Free Appropriate Public Education (FAPE) requirements.

Since 1975, every student with a disability is entitled to a Free Appropriate Public Education under the Individuals with Disabilities Act. (IDEA).

While the percentage of students receiving special education services continues to grow, the number of qualified candidates to support the growing need continues to decrease and most often impact students of color the most. The Learning Policy Institute (2017) wrote in the article entitled, "Teacher Turnover: Why it Matters and What We Can do About It," that schools with larger low-income student populations and higher populations of student-of-color have greater rates of teacher turnover in comparison to schools with different student populations. Thus, schools serving mainly low-income students and students of color are often subjected to a revolving door of less-experienced teachers. Thus, the need for innovative solutions to address the teacher shortage and teacher retention is essential.

Teachers with the least teaching credentials often teach students with the most critical educational needs. Last year, in California, nearly 60% of the special education teachers were enrolled in an alternative preparation program, according to EdSource (2020). This national crisis affects students throughout our nation.

Rural school districts face greater challenges in hiring special education teachers due to lower pay, geographic and social isolation, and teacher burnout due to teaching multiple subjects. School districts across the nation face the same challenge with recruiting and retaining special education teachers.

Preservice teachers often shy away from earning a degree in special education due to the pressures and demands in the classroom. According to an NPR (2015), special education teachers often cite feelings of isolation, fear of litigation, and student behaviors as the reasons for choosing not to pursue a degree in special education. While the research mentioned is over five years old, the reasons previously stated are still valid. In addition, teachers also face the fear of parent demands and failure to meet student's academic goals and objectives.

While, annually, school districts employ intensive recruitment strategies to recruit and retain quality special education teachers, statistics reveal that nearly 13% of special education teachers leave the profession annually. Recruitment strategies such as grow your own, referral incentives, signing bonuses, internships, and residencies have been added to the array of recruitment in the hopes of increasing the number of special education teachers hired each year.

Although the previously mentioned strategies have yielded success in the past, the number of students choosing to pursue education as a career has significantly declined over the past three years.

Personal Experience

"A good special education teacher is hard to find and even harder to hang on to." (Garcia-Navarro, n.d.).

Over the past thirty years of teaching special education students, supporting special education teachers as an administrator, and recruiting and retaining special education teachers as a Human Resources professional, the best memories were those of being a classroom teacher. Memories such as building relationships with students and watching them learn and grow have been my motivation throughout the years.

However, instances of fear and anxiety were often a part of my daily routine. Feelings of fear and anxiety stemmed from being a regular education teacher that taught special education students. I often wondered if I was doing enough to meet the students' needs according to their IEP goals and objectives. I soon realized that other teachers felt the same way. I felt that teachers who earned special education degrees were better prepared than we met student needs. I also noticed that teachers were leaving the profession feeling overwhelmed and defeated.

Many colleagues felt ill-prepared to handle student behaviors while meeting the increasing demands of student needs. A few times in my career, I wanted to leave the profession and start a new job, but I knew that teaching was my calling.

During one of my episodes of uncertainty, I met one of the most passionate special education teachers I have ever known. Her name was Roberta Bombo-Coleman. She exuded passion for her students and taught me all that she knew about special education. Her relationship with her parents and her ability to help me build the confidence I needed to help my students succeed. I visited her class often during my planning time. I observed, asked questions, and then practiced what I learned in my classroom.

Our conversations, collaborative sharing, and one-on-one professional development sessions stirred up my desire to support other teachers in building capacity as regular education teachers of special education students. I realized that the model Ms. Bombo-Coleman and I had stumbled upon was critical to helping other teachers.

Through this experience, I developed a desire to support other teachers and share the strategies and insight learned from Ms. Bombo-Coleman. When I transitioned to the role of an assistant principal, our administrative team worked with regular education teachers to build capacity. Our team assisted teachers with monitoring and working with other colleagues to ensure that teachers could help students achieve their best levels.

Despite the support and encouragement, teachers still left the profession, mentioning excessive paperwork, student behaviors, and parent complaints as reasons for leaving the teaching profession. Our team often stayed after school, listened, and encouraged teachers to stay. We noticed that the relationships, support, and collaboration caused a few teachers to stay each year. A few years later, I became a principal of an elementary school.

While my position changed, my collaboration and support model for regular education teachers of special education students had not. I quickly realized that I had found my tribe. Many of the teachers at the school were also sharing, supporting, and offering private and grade-level collaboration to help all teachers succeed.

For example, teachers ate lunch together while discussing the best ways to meet students' IEP goals. During the conversations, teachers decided if the best instructional model for the student would be taught in a collaborative or a small group setting based on the standard, students' prior knowledge, and the teacher's professional knowledge.

Fewer teachers left, and student achievement soared. As a community of learners, we knew that we had stumbled upon something great. As principal, I was fortunate to hire less than ten teachers during my three- and half-year tenure. I discovered that collaboration and teacher support were among the best recruiting and retention strategies for all teachers. I also noticed that very few special education teachers left the school. It was during my years as a principal that my desire to recruit and retain teachers was birthed.

A few years later, I became an HR Staffing Director at the district office. As an HR Staffing Director, I assisted schools with identifying the best teachers to fill vacant positions. I knew that relationships, professional development, collaboration, and support were primary keys to successfully recruiting and retaining special education teachers. Our metrics revealed that the number of preservice and alternative special education teachers slightly decreased. As a result, we realized that we needed to add additional staffing directors to assist with hiring special education teachers.

The Solution

The recruitment and retention of teachers capable of providing quality instruction while addressing educational equity and increasing achievement for all, including those with disabilities, is the core issue. A task this large calls for approaches and best practices that do not often align with what school districts have done in the past as they often carry a large price tag. Before looking at best practices, we must first explore this idea of "educational equity" if we believe all students deserve quality instruction.

In the article, *What is Resource Equity? A Working Paper that Explores the Dimensions of Resource Equity that Support Academic Excellence,* Jonathan Travers (2018) notes that "when we say 'equitable,' we do not mean that every individual student gets the same thing. Instead, we mean that we must provide all students with the resources required to create the kind of experiences they need to meet rigorous academic expectations and succeed in our fast-changing information- and technology-based society, so that race, income, and zip code no longer predict success in school and beyond."

This means that staffing Title I schools, schools with high percentages of students receiving free and reduced lunch, and schools with large populations of black and brown children is not acceptable if focused on educational equity.

Approaches such as internships and residencies are growing in popularity as they tend to yield positive outcomes for all students and staff. Residency programs offer opportunities for school districts to recruit teachers in critical fields, such as special education, math, and science, and targeted locations while giving candidates quality clinical preparation. The goal of teacher residencies is to provide solid training, mentoring, and help teachers build relationships early in their careers. Residency programs also offer financial incentives such as paying for degrees and paying teachers during their residencies to retain teachers for the duration of their careers.

While there are many ways to recruit and retain teachers, teacher residencies yield high returns and strategically address educational equity. By design, teacher residencies use a clinical approach, similar to medical residencies, where novice teachers are prepared in the school they will be assigned to teach. Residents are paired with experienced teachers during the residency period and receive a financial incentive.

The Learning Policy Institute, in the article, "Teacher Residencies, Building a High-Quality, Sustainable Workforce" (2017), determined key characteristics of a strong residency program:

1. Strong district/university partnerships

2. Coursework, which is integrated with the clinical practice

3. Full-year residency teaching alongside an expert mentor teacher

4. High-ability, diverse candidates recruited to meet specific district hiring needs (i.e., special education, math, science, bilingual, etc.)

5. Financial incentive tied to a three-four-year teaching commitment

6. Cohorts of residents placed in schools that model good practices with diverse learners

7. Expert mentor, teachers who co-teach with residents

8. Ongoing mentor and support for graduates

Impact of Residencies:

Residencies provide school districts an opportunity to increase gender and racial diversity in the teaching workforce. From 2000 to 2015, the percent of students enrolled in public schools who identify as students of color increased from 39 percent to over 50 percent (U.S. Department of Education, National Center for Education Statistics, 2017). However, school districts have found it difficult to recruit and retain teachers of color to reflect the diverse student populations. 80 percent of public school teachers are white (U.S. Department of Education, Office of Planning, Evaluation, and Policy Development, Policy and Program Studies Service, 2016).

Residencies can address the need for more diverse staff. According to the Learning Policy Institute, across teacher residency programs nationally, more than a third of residents (38 percent) in 2014-15 were people of color, double the national average of new teachers of color entering the field (19 percent). Residencies are one promising model to support the recruitment and retention of diverse staff ready to provide quality instruction to all students.

The statistics surrounding retention of teachers who participated in a residency model suggest the model supports retention many years after residents have exited from the program. According to the Learning Policy Institute, a study of graduates of the 12 oldest and largest residency programs found 82% still teaching in the same district in their third and fourth year, compared with 72% of non-residency recruits.

Decreasing turnover rates in schools can positively increase student achievement and increase the skill set of teachers.

This idea of teachers growing because participation in residencies is evident. The National Center for Teacher Residencies (NCTR) noted in "Impact of Resident-Mentor Pairs on Teacher Effectiveness" (December 2020), "hosting a resident in the classroom is positively associated with a higher teacher effectiveness score for the host teacher." What's more, The Learning Institute, in the review of the "Boston Teacher Residency," found that residency graduates surpass the effectiveness of new and veteran teachers in math after the fourth year of teaching." Thus, teaching residencies have the potential to increase the teacher pipeline and positively influence student achievement.

Gwinnett County Public Schools has recently implemented a promising model to support the recruitment and retention of high-quality special education teachers. The Special Education Internship Program was designed using the characteristics noted earlier by the Learning Policy Institute. The school district partners with local colleges and universities to recruit students interested in teaching special education. These students are placed with a mentor teacher for an established time and then transition to a teaching position upon completing the program. A commitment stipend is also provided to complete the internship and commitment to teaching special education in Gwinnett County Public Schools.

In addition to the Special Education Internship, Gwinnett County Public Schools has partnered with Georgia Gwinnett College (GGC) to build another pipeline of viable special education candidates through our Paraprofessionals to Bachelors Program. This program is a Grow Your Own Program.

Current Gwinnett County Public Schools paraprofessionals are provided an opportunity to pursue a Bachelor's degree in Special Education from GGC while still working as a paraprofessional. In this way, they continue to earn their salary and take classes on the weekends and/or online.

Targeting special education paraprofessionals is ideal because they already have experience with students with disabilities and usually only need the pedagogy and credentials to become a special educator. The program continues to grow and has provided the district another pipeline of prepared special education teacher candidates.

Our desire to recruit and retain special education teachers has caused our team to find creative solutions to meet the needs of our special education students. As an Associate Superintendent of Human Resources and Talent management, my personal goal is to provide robust professional development and as many collaboration opportunities as possible to retain our special education teachers.

I look forward to seeing the return on the investment of our residency programs. I believe that teachers possess a unique resilience and gift of helping others succeed. The pandemic has stretched teachers beyond their wildest dreams. Yet, they rose to the occasion this year and found ways to ensure that our students received a quality education, and I believe they will continue to do so. I also think that this is our finest hour. Our residency program is one way to ensure that teachers are adequately prepared and supported in meeting our students' needs.

References

- Carver-Thomas, D. & Darling-Hammond, L. (2017). Teacher turnover: Why it matters and what we can do about it. Palo Alto, CA: Learning Policy Institute.

- Garcia-Navarro, L. Qotebanner.com https://quotebanner.com/quotes/lourdes-garcianavarro-quote-21403/a-good-special-education-teacher-is-hard-to-find-and-even-harder-to-hang-on-to. Retrieved on May 4, 2021

- Guha, R., Klnl, T., (2016) Teacher Residencies, Building a High-Quality, Sustainable Workforce: Learning Policy Institute

- Hale, L., (2015, November 9) Behind the Shortage of Special Education Teachers: Long Hours, Crushing Paperwork, https://www.npr.org/sections/ed/2015/11/09/436588372/behind-the-shortage-of-special-ed-teachers-long-hours-crushing-paperwork

- Travers, J. What is Resource Equity? A working paper that explores the dimensions of resource equity that support academic excellence, Education Resource Strategies, http://www.erstrategies.org. Retrieved on May 4, 2021

"…All life is interrelated.
We are caught in an inescapable network
of mutuality; tied in a single garment of destiny.
Whatever affects one directly, affects all indirectly …
Strangely enough, I can never be what I ought to be
until you are what you ought to be.
You can never be what you ought to be
until I am what I ought to be."

Dr. Martin Luther King, Jr.

Evalaurene Jean-Charles
Middle School Teacher

My name is Evalaurene Jean-Charles, a recent graduate from the CUNY Baccalaureate for Unique and Interdisciplinary Studies program, where I studied the Sociology of Educational Inequity and Social Justice in Underserved Communities. Upon graduation, I joined Teach for America, as a 2020 New York City corp member, making me a first-year Special Education Teacher at a charter school in the South Bronx. In addition to my position as a teacher, I am the founder of Black on Black Education, which is an education consulting firm and soon-to-be non-profit organization that seeks to transform, revolutionize, reimagine, and recreate education in the Black Community by providing expert courses, conferences, and consulting so that Black students receive the education they deserve.

Eva@blackonblackeducation.com
www.blackonblackeducation.com

Eradicate Complacency

By Evalaurene Jean-Charles

Would "not right now" be a good enough answer if it was about your child's education? Would you remain complacent at the sight of clear and unacceptable injustice because it's easier to stay silent than to stand up and fight? Are you willing to wait until next year, or the year after, to better support students on their journey through life, or is the time for change RIGHT NOW? I think you know the answer.

Education comes from the root word "educere," which means "to bring up; to draw out." This means the foundation of our educational system should be finding and developing the intellectual treasure that lies inside of each and every one of our young people. Sadly, the state of our current system believes education means "to push in," which is the same premise since the start of the compulsory education system over 100 years ago.

Founders, like Horace Mann, had no intention of using it to push the status quo. In fact, they were creating it, not as a tool to fight for equity but as a tool of control. Although the content, length, and size of the system have changed, the use and the theoretical framework on which it was built remain the same. The system is committed to a culture of complacency, built on the belief that change must come slowly, and designed to create people full of sameness in a world of difference and diversity. It's past time to radically shift this paradigm.

The leaders of yesteryear created a system that too many leaders of today have chosen to follow. A position of complacency that can no longer be accepted. Too many maintain the mindset that systems are hard to change. Therefore, they assert that making small incremental reforms each year will be enough to face the harsh reality that this system is failing our children.

It's the difference between evolutionary and revolutionary change. When the latter is the only thing that can address the needs of the times in which we find ourselves. The time where students leave high school on 4th and 5th-grade reading levels, with undiagnosed or misdiagnosed learning disabilities, and worst of all, a belief that education cannot serve their path to success, must end.

So I ask you, is this the best that we can do when students, particularly those in low-income communities of color, are being told they aren't good enough or that they will never amount to anything? Is it the best we can do when special education students and English language learners are being taught by teachers without the tools or resources to support them? Complacency got us here!

As a first-year teacher, I came into the profession ready to change lives, but months later, I feel defeated and scared for the generations to come if drastic changes don't occur. Our education system is going to change because it has to change and the only way to do that is to recreate, reform, and revolutionize the entire system, rebuilding from the ground up.

Before even entering a classroom, I knew educational inequity existed but saw it firsthand during my junior year of undergraduate school. That's when I became a John Jay Vera Fellow and was assigned to work for a year at the Center for Alternative Sentencing and Employment Services in Brooklyn, New York. In my position there, I worked with young people between the ages of 14 and 25, who had large gaps in their education due to incarceration.

My job was to support them on their journey to passing their high school equivalency exam and increasing their personal and professional development. I created academic lessons, facilitated workshops, and secured guest speakers on financial literacy while curating fun events that promoted mental health and self-care. I was working with students close to my age and older that had been failed by the public education system.

The population of students I served had jobs, children, and family obligations which made attendance inconsistent, but on April 1st, 2019, I had a full house. I walked in with my lesson plan and my notes, ready to get to work as the students filed into the computer lab. I set up our music and played the This is Nipsey Hussle playlist on Spotify, as this was the day after his murder. Once we were five minutes into class and students got settled, as always, I checked in on how they were doing outside of their academics and the conversation of his death began.

I ran 2-3 hour sessions and that lesson I was prepared to teach was completely thrown out the window because, on that day, it wasn't what they needed. They needed to talk about the trauma that is watching one of their heroes die, the realities of gang violence, and the deep connection they felt with his life and his lyrics.

This was the day it became clear that I was meant to work in education, supporting youth in whatever capacity I could. This was the day that I realized students needed, not wanted, but needed to be able to bring their full selves into the classroom and by sticking to the status quo, they would never get that opportunity to do so, so I got to work.

My next step was transferring into the CUNY Baccalaureate for Unique and Interdisciplinary Studies Program, where I changed my major to the Sociology of Educational Inequity and Social Justice in Underserved Communities. Starting this course of study triggered the creation of my business Black on Black Education, an education consulting firm and soon-to-be non-profit organization that seeks to transform, revolutionize, reimagine, and recreate education in the Black Community by providing expert courses, conferences, and consulting so that Black students receive the education they deserve.

It was clear to me that eradicating the culture of complacency in our schools was needed in both the private and public sectors. Through our practice, we educate the public on the work that is anti-racism, and facilitate what Dr. Bettina Love calls "freedom dreaming" (2020) through our weekly podcast, clubhouse chats, Instagram lives, and the semi-annual Black on Black Education Conference.

Next, I applied to *Teach For America*, because upon graduation, I knew I wanted to teach as soon as possible and through this program, I would have that opportunity. Through research, I applied, knowing the realities of the program. I was aware that although its mission "one day all students will receive an equitable education," the program had issues that contribute to the inequality we see in schools all over the country, like placing teachers in schools that do not live into making this mission true, not adequately preparing teachers for the reality of the classroom, or school politics, and adding to the lack of stability and teacher turnover rate that cripples low-income communities.

Even so, I chose to use the program as a catalyst for a teaching career, remaining an activist, and fierce advocate for change. Now months into becoming a classroom teacher at a transfer school in the South Bronx, I have not wavered in my commitment to supporting the needs of Black students and students of color.

Educators, members of school leadership, and policymakers may read this and deny the plausibility of making the changes that right these wrongs on a day-to-day basis but through our work, it's become abundantly clear that collectively the blueprint for transformation exists. We discuss it every day with people in the trenches.

These coaches, consultants, and trainers from across the globe; help us focus on restorative practices, social-emotional learning, and anti-racism. Project-based learning experts assist Black on Black Education in creating conversations about how to use education as a tool for liberation.

Like many others, we spend countless hours outlining exactly what we need to know and be able to do to serve all students, eliminate the equity gap, and eradicate perpetuated complacency in the education system. Yet, schools across the country maintain the status quo, teach to the test and fail to do the work necessary to make the school system one that educates and liberates all.

So how do you, as an educator, school leader, non-profit employee, or activist, eradicate complacency in your work communities? Get to work! There are books, articles, videos, professional development, Tik Toks, Clubhouse chats, webinars, Instagram, and Facebook lives chalked full of the answers to the question everyone in the system should be asking, *How do I individually, and as part of a collective, provide students with the education we would want to be provided to our own kids?*

The answer, in my experience, the only way is to implement policies and practices that don't leave room for satisfaction in the existing condition of the education system is to start with setting professional goals for yourself and for your students, collaborate often with educators who are also committed to innovation. Remember the reasons in which you became an educator and be honest with yourself about the habits you must form to maintain your commitments and reach your professional goals. More importantly, guide students toward identifying and achieving theirs.

The well-researched and well-practiced strategy that helps me remain innovative and maintain my commitment to the needs of the students of color that I serve is maintaining and growing as an anti-racist practitioner committed to social justice education. Complacency in the education system is a slap in the face of social justice. It is a direct descendant of the current goals and objectives for student learning, which are rooted in a hegemonic white-dominant framework.

When more educators begin to adopt holistic ways of teaching, they begin to step into an innovative classroom, not dictated by lesson plans, but by the individual needs and lived experiences of the students. Being an anti-racist practitioner requires that I actively question my practices and behaviors, build strong relationships with my students and families and embrace what Paulo Freire calls a "problem-posing education," which recognizes that students have the knowledge and that education should not be a commodity transferred from teacher to student but a "practice of freedom"; (Freire, 1970), necessary to understand theory and skills as well as embrace interconnectedness and critical thinking.

The education system will not be dismantled tomorrow or the day after that, but becoming an anti-racist practitioner, embracing problem-posing education (Freire, 1970), and implementing social justice education (Hackman, 2005) makes it impossible to remain complacent with the state of education.

Where do we go from here? The coronavirus pandemic has provided us with a unique opportunity to do things differently and way too many have opted to stick to the status quo. Using this time to maintain the old system online rather than learn from the mistakes of the past, and move forward with an innovative mindset that decenters the teacher, values the opinions of students, and creates learning communities not centered around a test but around learning the skills and building the tools necessary to be holistically well.

With the wealth of knowledge available and the stakes so high, shame on each and every one of us if we walk back into classroom business as usual. Question your practice, move forward committing to the needs of students, and let's build a better future together by committing not to the system but to the rights and needs of all students.

References

- Freire, Paulo, and Donaldo Macedo. Pedagogy of the Oppressed: 50th Anniversary Edition. 4th ed., Bloomsbury Academic, 2018.

- Hackman, Heather W. "Five Essential Components for Social Justice Education." *Equity & Excellence in Education*, vol. 38, no. 2, 2005, pp. 103–09. *Crossref*, doi:10.1080/10665680590935034.

- Love, Bettina. *We Want to Do More Than Survive: Abolitionist Teaching and the Pursuit of Educational Freedom*. Illustrated, Beacon Press, 2020.

Dr. Marie Hubley-Alcock
Futurist Educator

Marie Hubley-Alcock, Ph.D., is a futurist educator and thought leader. She has authored and co-authored a number of books in the field of education on topics such as; contemporary curriculum design, meaningful assessment practices, questing and engaging instructional practices, the future of education systems and policy, game design in the classroom, virtual interdependent thinking in humans, standards-based practices, and education technology in classrooms.

Dr. Alcock has also participated in the foundation of and running of several educational companies and non-profit organizations, including Learning Systems Associates, which is a national and international consulting firm and Tomorrow's Education Network, which is a non-profit dedicated to promoting classical and contemporary literacy development for students.

Dr. Alcock has been a teacher and administrator in private and public schools for over 25 years. She has been a professor at Walden University. She is an active advocate for learners of all ages and has said the "science of teaching is an invitational art." She is known for describing a quality curriculum as "one with balance between guaranteed non-negotiables and personalized, joyful, career inspiring experiences that can make the world a better place."

www.lsalearning.com

The New Teacher Job Description

By Dr. Marie Hubley-Alcock

M any teachers today began in a career educated to behave as it was expected in the industrial model and then "poof" they are asked to be a contemporary teacher for contemporary students. My job as a teacher trainer is to support these teachers in developing new teaching practices. However, the teachers feel as if the rug has been pulled out from them, and in some cases, even betrayed by their profession. They thought they understood what was expected of them, but it has changed over the past 25 years – dramatically.

The issue is, the education system is changing, but the teacher job description has not been updated since 1906, when the NEA Committee of Ten met in New York and updated it to reflect the needs of the industrial age. They created the separation of subjects like math and social studies and English as well as grouping children by age.

The time has come for us to gather again as a profession and reflect on the needs of the contemporary students and design a job description that makes sense for the way the job looks now. Teachers today feel overwhelmed and under supported as they try to balance the different policies, expectations, and needs of the students they are dedicated to educating. We need to be honest about what the job of a teacher is, so we attract people who are eager to embrace the unique challenges and rewards that come with the position.

The challenge is that we must engage with existing staff to grow the capacity to be a contemporary profession. When I began my career, I was trained to write unit plans and lesson plans and I was given the task to make learning fun. "I want kids to learn without even realizing they are learning" was something I would say in 1995.

I had my paper grade book, and I organized my classes into quarters and used the 100-point scale to reward students who completed my tasks or catch the students who did not. After each report card, I would have parent conferences to discuss goals and the performance of children with their families. We had one professional development day a year and we would have a speaker come to teach us something helpful. The review of curriculum would be on a five-year rotation.

Let's fast forward to today. Teachers are more like doctors than factory workers. The goal now is to educate every student, in everything, to the highest level possible in the least restrictive environment. Teachers are aligning to standards and creating tasks that are precise enough for diagnosing exactly what the student should be working on to improve their work.

This kind of feedback is expected to be ongoing throughout the learning process, every day if possible. Teachers are working with students over video screens and through online learning platforms. Gradebooks are online and parents can monitor the results daily. The industrial model of education is coming to an end. The information model of education is here.

When I work with schools today, we have conversations about "making bold moves" based on the book *Bold Moves: Designing Remarkable Learning Environments,* which I co-authored with Heidi Hayes Jacobs and was published by ASCD in 2017. By "bold moves," we mean things like designing contemporary curriculum and assessments or teaching methods. We also discuss changing schedules, school architecture, how we group students, even how we group teachers.

The idea is to shift away from assigning one teacher to a group of children and expecting that one teacher, in isolation, to be all things to all children. This kind of "bold move" is possible and there are many ways to make it happen.

My concern is that teachers and school leaders are asked to make these "bold moves" without any attention to how this will change their roles as teachers. Suddenly they need to teach students to be aware of their own learning process and be able to self-navigate their own learning. Teachers quickly need to be fluent in digital, media, and global literacy.

I have had a teacher say to me in the middle of a training session, "I would love to do these things, but no one has taught me HOW to do them!" These things cannot be taught in one professional development day a year. So, that means teachers need to be continuous learners too. It is the only way to stay cutting-edge in the practices that work. Getting a degree and then doing a student teaching experience is just not enough to prepare us for a thirty-year career.

So, I work with teams of teachers every day, training them to be able to make "bold moves," and here, I am calling for a new job description, so teachers know exactly what being a teacher really entails. Teachers want to do the work, but they deserve to know what the job entails before they sign on the dotted line. So, this is my suggestion for the job description.

Imagine we are in a school that is about to hire for the next year. We are putting a posting out and this is what it says.

We are looking for a self-motivated and engaging teacher with a passion for learning. As a teacher, you will be responsible for cultivating the students' passions and interest in education and their own development. Your responsibilities will include the following roles:

1. Teacher as self-navigating professional learner

2. Teacher as nurturer and listener

3. Teacher as expert on child development and human learning process

4. Teacher as advocate for learners

5. Teacher as assessor of needs at a diagnostic and prescriptive level for all students

6. Teacher as plant and safety supervisor

7. Teacher as knowledge and skill source

8. Teacher as communication link between families/students and the school

9. Teacher as researcher and project manager

10. Teacher as facilitator and presenter

11. Teacher as caring disciplinarian

12. Teacher as a networker and collaborator

13. Teacher as innovator and designer

14. Teacher as media critic, media maker, and publisher

15. Teacher as global citizen

This list requires a tremendous range of skills and dispositions. Just being knowledgeable about a specific discipline is not enough to be an effective teacher. In my experience, teachers have been proficient in parts of this list while frustrated or untrained in other parts. The first phase of the solution is to support school systems in asking for exactly what they really need through an updated job description.

The second phase of the solution is to have teacher preparation programs that teach and support teachers in all these areas. The third phase of the solution is to have teachers work to develop these skills and dispositions in students, so they are prepared for their own futures. Let us go through each one briefly.

Teacher as a self-navigating professional learner – this is the ability to learn independently and stay current on topics related to the profession of education. This means organizing our own learning as teachers and not waiting for the district to provide all the needed professional development. It also means modeling the process of learning for students.

Children need models who can be transparent about what to do when we do not understand an idea or have questions. As the professional teacher in the room, we are called to be the professional learner.

Teacher as nurturer and listener – this is the ability to care and support all students and families that are members of the school community. Many schools today have a bad habit of imposing culture and middle-class values on the community. Although this is a classic role, it needs a contemporary upgrade to include listening with compassion and understanding. It also means being reflective about our own biases and culture so that we can be self-aware as a listener to anyone beyond our own experiences. Teachers, like doctors, are there to help, not judge.

Teacher as expert on child development and human learning process – this is the ability to identify what is developmentally appropriate for a group of learners. Brains are developing differently now, and teachers need to be aware of the impacts of sound system development and the visual cortex development on everything from teaching reading to how we decorate the classroom.

These kids do not need more visual stimulation and we must reduce the clutter in our classrooms. These are simple things that will help contemporary students focus and feel ready to learn. In addition, we tend to move on too quickly without letting children experience a sense of success. This leads to brain fatigue and ultimately to lost instructional time.

Teacher as advocate for learners – this is the participation in the narrative about education in general as well as being loyal to learning as a process. Teachers are the defenders of the learning process. When we understand how people learn, then it is our job to protect their process and autonomy. An advocate also means defending the process of learning, which includes being able to struggle and fail in a safe environment because it is a natural part of learning. For example, if a school averages grades, they are in danger of punishing students who simply take longer to learn.

227

Teacher as assessor of needs at a diagnostic and prescriptive level for all students – this is the need for assessment to be short, precise, accurate, and meaningful. The work being done around standards-based assessments is helpful here and teachers should be fluent in assessment designs. Every assessment ever given to a learner should be able to give specific prescriptive information about what they should be working on to improve their performance. If it is not clearly aligned to a learning target, then we should ask why we are giving this assessment.

Teacher as plant and safety supervisor – this is a classic role but still vital for today. Protecting the health and wellbeing of children is complicated. Physical safety is straightforward enough but now includes protecting students from threats internal and external. We also consider the social and emotional needs of the learners and the kind of learning environments we are maintaining for them.

There are health needs like nutrition, sleep, and exercise. Finally, the moral and spiritual development of the child so they have balanced practices and can make healthy self-care choices for life. We have curriculums now that are dedicated to these elements that were never a part of the programs years ago.

Teacher as knowledge and skill source – this is a classic role, but the method of teaching them has evolved. It is not enough to be a dispenser of knowledge like a pitcher filling a willing cup with water. The teacher now needs a sophisticated tool kit of instructional strategies, including inquiry, grouping, lecture, demonstration, questing, and personalizing experiences so students can share and learn about things they care about and can connect to in a meaningful way.

Teachers are required to think about the knowledge they know but be open to the things students know as well. This is the beginning of a co-created curriculum and allows students to participate in school as a valid expert in their own experiences and interests. Personalization is the recognition of students as sources of knowledge and skills as well.

Teacher as communication link between families/students and the school – this role has also evolved over time to include 24/7 access to information about the learning process through websites and learning management systems. It goes deeper when we think about report cards and how they are no longer the best way to communicate about a student's progress.

Portfolios and self-navigation tools are used now to share gallery style evidence of work, process pieces that are focused on the steps taken to learn, and finally, progress elements that include before and after elements so families can celebrate growth.

This also ties back to being a good listener. As a communication link, the teacher is asked to really think about the experiences of a student away from school. Is there trauma? Is there food security? Is there a support structure or access to the supplies? These things impact learners and must be handled with compassion and free of judgement.

Teacher as researcher and project manager – staying on top of best practices and cutting-edge techniques requires a bit of research. Teachers are also experiencing changes in populations and the introduction of new challenges. Being dedicated to reliable research allows us as a profession to learn and grow with the community we are in. The role of a project manager is seen in both the organization and flow of the learning environment as well as the skill taught to learners. Students are asked to participate in project-based learning, problem-based learning, and phenomenon-based learning – they need a professional project manager to model time management and resource management.

Teacher as planner, facilitator, and presenter – the need to be engaging is classic. The quality of a facilitator or a presenter is the strength of their planning. Teaching has become a front-heavy profession, meaning we need to plan out individualized programs, differentiated programs, and so many pathways for students to reach success that we are then able to spend our time during the year working directly with students. Teachers are facilitators of a dynamic group of learners and so they are called to be dynamic and energetic enough to keep up. In addition, teachers are required to know when to stop giving all the answers and let the students wrestle with ideas on their own. The ability to balance facilitation and presentation is the art and science of being a teacher.

Teacher as caring disciplinarian – this is the need to provide structure. However, structure must come with kindness and patience. The goal is to impart students with an understanding of the role of structure and the ability of structure to protect the group and the individual. It is not about judging or punishing an offender. Learning restorative practices and ways to provide discipline with dignity are required now. As teachers, we care first and coach on behavior second. The social-emotional needs of students are paramount for successful learning.

Teacher as a networker and collaborator – this is one of the biggest changes for me. Teachers are not alone anymore. It is important to team – that has been around now for twenty years. Now we also network with the community businesses, create partnerships with specialized organizations like NASA, reach out to create field study programs and credentialing options for our students. We want to be networked with other schools, global classrooms, and professionals if we hope to provide a model of safe, effective, and efficient networking for our students.

Teacher as innovator and designer – this is the most exciting change for our profession. Our creativity is unleashed. We are asked to design curriculum experiences and learning spaces that are customized to the needs and interests of our students. This is why I say, "teaching is an invitational art." We get to design an invitation for our students that motivates them to engage personally with their own learning.

The challenge to teachers today is to create units that have topics, themes, issues, challenges, and case studies that are worthy of a student's effort. If our units of study do not create an opportunity for joy, a career, or the opportunity to make the world a better place, then we must ask why are we teaching this unit? I believe school is the real world for students, so we as teachers are challenged to respect that and not teach them things that "they might need someday later." Canned, regurgitated material is unacceptable now. We are all curriculum designers and innovative creators of learning experiences.

Teacher as media critic, media maker, and publisher – this is the world we live in today. Students are surrounded by media – they have access, but that does not make them proficient at it. In other words, how are they learning to critique what they see on a screen, think about the source and editing, ask questions about the biases included? As media makers, students are able to publish content without a gatekeeper. Who is teaching them how to make content that is high quality?

Teachers have media tools on their computers and laptops. It is part of the job to be capable of working through these tools and model everything from effective searches of the internet to producing quality podcasts and webisodes. We live in a world of information saturation and it is now part of the job to teach students how to navigate this world.

Teacher as global citizen – we are all members of communities and teachers are called to share the concept of the global community with students. It is more than being aware of the world or participating in a video conference with a group in a different country. The challenge is to teach students to think globally, communicate globally, recognize different perspectives, and take action.

For example, an eighth-grade teacher might have a group of students revise an essay for a global audience. This might mean revising for translation by removing introductory phrases. In a first-grade room, students might sit and hear stories read from grandmothers all around the world using the "global grandmothers' network." In addition, teachers are learning about education for sustainability which means systems thinking and the ability to think about global issues and generate potential solutions. Taking action to wrestle with current global issues is one of the finest things teachers can do with students of any age.

Every aspect of the teaching job has evolved and grown to be more complicated. Our role as teachers has developed layers and sub-roles that invite us to challenge the antiquated job descriptions. The skills and dispositions listed here have slowly and steadily become common parts of the daily, monthly, and yearly tasks of teachers at all grade levels.

The job has changed. It has become a true profession. We can meet this with courage and confidence. Let me see a teacher on the morning news challenging the world by saying, "give me any 25 students and watch what I can do in ten months. They will ALL be at standard or beyond."

If we are clear about this evolution of the job with teachers, I have no doubt we will be able to embrace these changes and be a contemporary profession. One that can meet today's challenges and prepare young learners for their unpredictable and complex future in the information age. I am deeply proud of teachers and our profession. We deserve clarity and a common voice describing what the career is and how we can lead it together.

Ben Bruhn
High School Social Studies Teacher

Ben Bruhn is a high school social studies, AVID, and credit recovery teacher at St. Helens High School in St. Helens, Oregon. He is also an adjunct instructor at Portland State University, where he coteaches the social studies methods courses to future teachers. He grew up in Seattle and did community development work around the USA and overseas before earning his MAT at the University of Washington in 2012 with endorsements in social studies, language arts, and ESOL. He is a National Board Certified Teacher who has worked in a wide range of school settings. He has earned his administrative license and is in the process of completing a Master of Science in Ed. from Portland State University. His desire to help bridge cultural divides and his love for collaboration drives him to engage with all levels of the educational community to foster and advocate for student-centered engagement. Follow him on Instagram @Ben.Bruhn.

Initiating a Grassroots Equity Movement Focused on Race Relations

By Ben Bruhn

I believe a school's primary strength is the quality and longevity of relationships between staff, students, families, and the community. Events in recent memory have brought constant and quick changes to our way of life at school. The 2016 presidential election, protests related to race, and COVID19 restrictions have collectively exposed and amplified a longstanding skepticism and fear of outside influence and ideas.

Many personal stories accompany these events--the closing of the last lumber mill, parents and students chanting "Build the Wall" during football games, police intervening on campus between students and between parents when demonstrations turned violent, racial assaults during basketball games, and people defying government orders to "mask up" due to believing it's all a hoax.

All of this puts school leaders in a tough position. My school community is very supportive: they volunteer, establish programs, and they even passed a generous bond measure in the midst of this pandemic. Yet, they also express a strong desire to keep the status quo, believing that preserving the comfort of the majority is more important than addressing the discomfort and oppression of the minority.

Advocating for equity has felt to many like a threat to equality and creates a defensiveness about being held accountable for one's actions. For example, several incidents occurred that met the legal definition of racism and bigotry, yet those involved adamantly denied "being racist" or that race had anything to do with it. Many in the community and staff believe that being colorblind is the solution because individual relationships are what will "fix racism." There is hesitance to acknowledge problems, denial in not seeing oneself as part of the problem, and resistance to pursuing equitable actions to address the problems.

When I joined my current school district in the fall of 2018, I did not see myself as a leader. I was simply grateful to be seen as an asset instead of a liability. In my previous district, I met a lot of resistance for implementing basic practices of good teaching: teaching skills, designing engaging lessons and incorporating student voice. My approach was seen as a threat to the school culture, which promoted compliance over connection.

In my new district, my approach was celebrated, and I was encouraged to join new teams, one of which was our district social studies curriculum adoption committee. Our team had a wonderful blend of experience and expertise, and I appreciated their candidness about the dilemmas in selecting and implementing a new curriculum. They knew teachers needed training in both the content and pedagogy of social studies but also in how to handle the discomfort of being asked to shift their practices and teach new state standards around ethnic studies, tribal history, and the Holocaust and genocide.

Many of our colleagues said they just wanted a new curriculum, but it was clear we all needed meaningful professional development. It reminded me of the needs I saw in the teacher education program where I was an adjunct instructor—candidates loving the content but being hesitant to see and disrupt their assumptions about students and education. No curriculum could solve the problem of an unhealthy learning environment.

This is when my initial vision for an equity team began and it motivated me to get my administrative license. I wanted to be equipped to see and engage with the larger systems of our district. I entered a program that summer and joined six different teams as a way to build relationships across and within various school systems and immediately saw a pattern of incoherent visions and mixed messages from administrators about how to operate and move forward. In both my graduate classes and practicum, I was being shown how to manage but not how to lead.

SPRING

When my school initially closed for two weeks in March 2020, it gave me time to begin synthesizing all that I had been trying to wrap my head around through my various roles and passions. As a teacher, I knew there was an overwhelming amount of practices that needed to be implemented under the umbrella of equity (culturally responsive teaching, trauma-informed care, restorative practices, etc.).

Administrators spent most of their time addressing behavior concerns which left them functioning more as managers instead of leaders. Most teachers relied on the voluntary efforts of others to do the majority of the work in shifting the culture to address student needs. There were a lot of gaps between stated visions and lived realities. I found the same to be true in higher education, which is why I revamped the social studies methods courses in a teacher education program which I co-taught as an adjunct instructor. I wanted to equip educators, both at my school and the university, to engage with the pressing issues of the modern classroom.

As someone who wants to see the "big picture," I reached out to educators across the nation to get input and advice on how and where to begin in pursuing equity. I had a lot of ideas and questions floating in my head and I needed time to see and feel where they connected with my heart, my "why." This introspection may be the first step in addressing the thoughts, behaviors, and assumptions that divide people in this country.

I became a teacher because I wanted all students to feel like they belonged, were seen, celebrated, and valued. Without this, it's easy to start questioning your self-worth, value and purpose. For most of my career, I focused on doing this through adapting my curriculum to the students and shaping a healthier classroom culture. But in recent years, I had seen how essential it was for me to shift the culture outside of my classroom for students to truly feel a sense of belonging at the school.

The pandemic made it very clear how much the world outside of my classroom impacted my students' lived experiences—especially given the continual murder of black people (Breonna Taylor, Ahmaud Arbery, George Floyd, etc.). This horrified so many people and made us question the value of black lives in our country. In many ways, it seemed like my response and those of other white people were often similar to witnessing a car accident — initial shock and then a quick return to "normalcy."

But because I had become increasingly aware of how people of color, especially black and indigenous people, have been oppressed throughout our history, I was more open to seeing racism as a system, rather than simply as individual evil acts. But seeing it as a system meant I could no longer distance myself from it. I had to see that I was connected to the problem and had a responsibility to confront it. It wasn't enough to just not be racist. I needed to be antiracist.

I needed to see how the problem was not "out there" with "those people" but actually with me. I needed to be vulnerable and have the courage to see the darkness inside me. If I could learn to confront and dismantle my racist ideas and actions, then I would be more capable of confronting and dismantling the racism in my environment. I decided to listen and learn from others who could help orient me to the work of antiracism.

Ibram Kendi reminded me that racist and antiracist identities are not fixed as a good/bad binary as if I were either perfect or evil, but rather it was a daily choice between denial and confession: "the heartbeat of racism is denial. The heartbeat of antiracism is confession." Layla Saad called me out on wanting to look like I was "one of the goods ones" by saying, "Your desire to be seen as good can actually prevent you from doing good, because if you do not see yourself as part of the problem, you cannot be part of the solution."

(Saad, 2020, p. 143) Austin Channing Brown helped me see how the work of antiracism was really an invitation to experience a more full humanity.

But the only reason my mind was open to a shift in consciousness was because I had already begun the work of dismantling specific white supremacy norms, like perfectionism, the right to comfort, and fear of conflict. One example of this is how my own fragility and the pressure from my administrators to mitigate discomfort or disagreement in class led me to quickly intervene after heated exchanges between students. I would often end up choosing to prioritize the comfort of one student over another student's comfort, focusing on intent over impact.

My fear of conflict, desire for comfort, and the pressure to "get it right" (perfectionism) prevented me from handling situations appropriately, especially if it involved race. Similar to my definition of racism, I had to expand my definition of white supremacy beyond the narrow idea of violent right-wing extremists. It was a whole system designed to maintain whiteness as "normal" and the standard for "the ways things are."

Learning to see racism as a system helped me see that white fragility was really part of a larger fragility around any uncomfortable topic, particularly when it related to a potential sense of responsibility. We so quickly are triggered by discomfort that almost any feedback is received as a personal attack on our character, value and worth. This makes sense when I considered how most white people see emotions as a liability, as something to stuff away, cover, and even deny.

It's no surprise then that many white educators are skeptical of restorative practices and rarely value emotional literacy, let alone model it. It was helpful to hear and read Brene Brown share her research on shame and vulnerability and hear her talk with Marc Brackett about how his research on emotional intelligence intersects with it (Brown, Daring Greatly, 2012 and Brackett, Permission to Feel, 2019). I had been digging into these issues to build emotional awareness, acceptance, and resilience in my personal life for years. I had been grappling with self-worth, self-compassion and authenticity to combat perfectionism which I now realized equipped me to be vulnerable and courageous in building the racial stamina necessary to engage with the lifelong work of antiracism.

SUMMER AND FALL

Taking time to internally process all of this March through June gave me the clarity I needed before moving forward with my dream of starting an equity movement in my district. It showed my need to commit to major internal "heart" work and that I needed to be authentic and vulnerable in inviting others into that work as well.

The staff hesitance, denial and resistance I had identified earlier related to problem-solving was certainly influenced by extreme autonomy and an unhealthy organizational culture, but now I saw that at the core was a systemic fragility that went beyond just discussions of race. I believed we needed to focus on race because if we could learn to process our discomfort, insecurities and denial about race, we'd be more able to process all of that with every other issue under the equity "umbrella." We had to be willing to make people uncomfortable to build the emotional stamina to process our own feelings and the feelings of others. We can't show empathy if we refuse to feel. We can't fix problems we pretend don't exist.

I had already been having conversations with our superintendent off and on for months, but we both knew I needed to grow things organically for them to be meaningful and sustainable. After finding personal clarity about the "heart" work I knew was necessary in any equity movement, I reached out to people I had already built relationships with across the district. And I felt truly blessed to have a veteran educator respond to me immediately and offer to partner with me in leading this movement! She invited me to join her in a coaching academy the next year that would be led by our state educator union.

The timing felt serendipitous because she found out about it the same day I sent her an email and both opportunities came at a time of great personal angst as she was processing the murder of George Floyd. We talked on the phone for hours over the next week and made plans to pitch our vision for forming an equity team to every school in our district. We shared our "why" behind starting this to give a vulnerable and powerful call to join us in forming a collective vision for equity.

Within a week, over 70 people expressed interest, representing 20% of our staff! We were able to meet with our school board and garnered some support for our work. We also had our district administrative team agree to set aside an hour slot every Friday for all staff to meet in small equity groups to dig into certain topics. From this larger group, my partner and I were able to identify and form a core group. We enjoyed hearing their personal "why" behind joining, their hopes, fears, and passion for equity.

It was a powerful experience and we met weekly with this core group through October with the primary goal of designing and supporting the equity groups who met on Fridays. So many people were excited to have conversations and share ideas for action, but time was limited, so we all decided to restructure our team in November to have more clarity and consistency with moving the work forward.

WINTER

It was freeing and exciting to share my passion with others on a range of levels and pour into people who wanted to learn and grow. It was encouraging to be affirmed as a leader who not only provided organization and structure but also authenticity and wisdom. It was time-consuming—I was easily spending 10 hours a week on this work in addition to my time commitment with our union's coaching academy and another academy we began with two of our core team members. My connection with my co-lead was invaluable because we spoke almost daily to reflect, share, and plan together.

In mid-November, it was a joy to connect as a new core team of nine people who represented almost every building in the district and brought a range of experiences. Our main challenge was that the groups were composed almost entirely of white people who were not fully aware of our blind spots related to race. This is why we wanted a coach but did not have the support from the district or our regional network to get one. But we continued meeting at least once each week to engage with and align our vision for equity on a variety of organizational levels.

It was great to begin by celebrating what was already starting to happen with equity in schools across our district. We shared our dreams for our team—to have the courage to face our discomfort in ourselves and in our community and to be the "go-to" team for students and staff who may be struggling with inequity. After initially brainstorming possible reasons why staff have a weak understanding of racial equity and why students of color are experiencing racial bias and inequity in school, we drafted questions to use in talking to staff and students about race. As we saw more of the complexity of how our positionality would influence our interviews, we realized we needed to focus on our team instead of larger groups of people.

Together, we analyzed why our group struggled to identify and counter racism in ourselves and our environment. After an initial brainstorm, we categorized the feedback:

- We don't fully understand socialization

- Our opinions and views on race are limited and uninformed

- Limited exposure to BIPOC

- Our definition of racism is too narrow

- We don't see ourselves in racial terms

- We deny and/or resist seeing our white supremacy culture

- We struggle to acknowledge and process discomfort

Our overall goal was to identify and understand our racial identity to counter racism in ourselves and our environment. As a team, we had talked about liking the head, heart, hands model to humanize our work:

- Develop critical consciousness to see racism in ourselves and our environment (HEAD)

- Learn/create and practice strategies to address our fatigue/fragility (HEART)

- Begin countering racism in our environment (people and systems) (HANDS)

This led us to do an identity marker activity in which we debriefed by each sharing one story about a time when one of the identity markers made us feel different. It was powerful to read each other's stories and identify which emotions came up. We then compared the emotions to ones we identified in a series of vignettes from "The Guide for White Women Who Teach Black Boys." We spent an entire meeting talking about the tricky subjectivity with the task of identifying emotions, which was very beneficial because it helped us all be more conscious about how we each label and process emotions.

For our next empathy interview, we shared about a time when we saw racial inequity: What did it sound like, look like, feel like? How did the experience make you feel? Did the experience impact you in any way? Was there any resolution? We had such a range of experiences and many of them happened outside of classrooms which reminded us of the need to do antiracist work in every area of our schools. It also motivated us to take time to identify each team member's strengths and affirm ways we were already making a difference in our immediate context.

Whenever we talked about making our work sustainable, we brought up the need for future building equity coordinators to have strong partnerships with their building administrators. With that in mind, I created a document summarizing how the deeper obstacles in the "soil" of our organizational culture reinforces the characteristics of white supremacy, which in turn reinforce the defensive claims that come from the process of white fragility around any topic that brings discomfort, especially race but not limited to race.

There is a general problem with all of our systems being designed to promote compliance over connection and a sense of fear over a sense of belonging. Because I knew that emotional literacy was a key antidote necessary for this work, I sought out experts who could help us to embed emotional intelligence into the curriculum and culture of schools. I also connected with those who could offer support to our administrators and leaders to equip them to engage in the deeper internal work necessary for systemic change and to authentically model and support their staff and students in it as well.

Committed to my own personal development, I sought educators outside of my district who were involved in the work of antiracism. But instead of processing in solitude, I formed authentic relationships with educators across the nation, the majority of whom are not white. That all began by joining Teachers for Good Trouble, a group focused on reforming learning environments to build safe, nurturing, and justice-driven academic communities, by advocating for legislation, policies, and resources that center the well-being of students, teachers, and learning communities.

My new "tribe" helped me explore new ways of using my privilege and positionality to advocate for equity and raise awareness about racial injustice. I had an interview with a radio station to raise awareness around the problems with standardized testing. Engaging with educators through Instagram and Clubhouse led me to amazing leaders who challenged and inspired me to find my purpose and use my voice for service, not self-promotion.

Especially after the insurrection at the Capitol Building, I was challenged to be a co-conspirator in antiracist work by speaking more directly to white people. It moved me to start initiating hard conversations around race with people I never knew and showing up with curiosity and a willingness to confess my mistakes and journey with unlearning and learning. In February, I decided to make social media posts every day dedicated to helping white people see and process their whiteness.

I started inviting people to form a book group on me and white supremacy by Layla Saad. Around that same time, I was interviewed on a podcast to talk about how I decenter whiteness in my work as an adjunct instructor in a teacher education program. All these opportunities felt like an expanded network of accountability that pushed me to take a stronger stance with my equity work in the district.

SPRING

My conversations with friends and strangers outside of my district gave me clarity and confidence in taking more bold steps with my antiracist work. A new friend invited me to join a panel at his conference in April on "Remixing Education," which helped me connect with others doing antiracist work in higher education. I continued sharing with my core team how much I was still uncovering about my whiteness. And it was humbling for me to realize how I was still sometimes unconsciously centering whiteness. Those mistakes were opportunities for me to choose confession instead of denial, to prioritize impact over intent, and invite stronger accountability instead of getting more defensive.

They also helped us start a discussion about specific behaviors that support or detract from our values. Processing this revealed my lingering white supremacy norms of "fear of conflict" and "I'm the only one" but also helped me, and others, see the power of their antidotes in calling us to build, instead of simply dismantle. It reminded me of a quote I had been returning to since the summer from Sharon Daloz Parks "Those who practice leadership for equity must confront, disappoint, and dismantle while at the same time energize, inspire, and empower." (Parks, 2005, p. 210)

Our core team, the Antiracist Educators, was not only bonding through our commitment to do the internal work, but we were also seeing ourselves and being seen by others as leaders. I was seeing myself become more of the bold, empathetic leader I had longed to be, and it came by leading more with my heart than my head. It was exciting for me to creatively weave in the need for emotional awareness and a shift in consciousness as we developed monthly workshops on racial equity open to all district staff.

The first one was "How We Show Up: Seeing Our Identities," which focused on raising staff awareness of their own identity markers and their intersectionality. It was powerful to have members of our team share their own experience in working through the temptation to deny the impact of socialization and fear of being "boxed in." By focusing on being curious about the personal stories "behind" each marker, it helped staff see the problem in being "blind" to them all.

Our second one was "Seeing the Construction of Race," and again, it helped to have our team lead with vulnerability in sharing how much we didn't know and had to learn. I was glad that about 15% of our staff came considering the high fragility around race. And the fact that most were engaged in sharing the emotional impact of seeing racism as a system instead of just individual action seemed to be proof of the trust that had been established with those who had been coming every Friday to the equity groups.

Between meetings, it was also encouraging to hear people share about how more people were talking about equity issues in their schools. Amid uncertainty and strain due to the pandemic and a stressful reopening of the buildings, we had kept momentum and there was excitement about the infrastructure we were developing to continue next year.

Our core team has committed to the "heart" work of antiracism and we know that we need help. It is exciting for us to imagine what is in store for our district as we craft job descriptions for building equity coordinator positions, begin meeting with leaders to shape our next district strategic plan, and design differentiated professional development for next year. We have done a lot of work, yet in many ways, the work is just beginning.

Dr. Cathy Owens-Oliver
Leadership Effectiveness Coach

DrCathyO is a master teacher, thought leader, and visionary author. She earned her doctoral degree in Education, Leadership, Management and Policy at Seton Hall University, where her dissertation addressed the negative impact of licensure testing on the minority teacher candidate pool. She is a National Board Certified Teacher in Early Adolescence English Language Arts. She has expertise in teacher preparation, education policy, school and teacher leadership, and cultural responsiveness.

She is the CEO of Educational Effectiveness Group, where she and her team provide coaching and consulting to schools and colleges of education. She has held senior roles at Educational Testing Service, Learning Forward, and the National Board for Professional Teaching Standards.

She is the best-selling author of *Why Schools Fumble: Helping Principals, Teachers, and Parents Identify and Solve Their School's Biggest Problems.* She has presented at many national conferences and written for leading education journals, including *Accomplished Teacher* Magazine, the *Journal of Staff Development*, and the Hope Foundation's *What Works in Schools*. Her work also appears in the college textbook: *Black Star: An Introduction to African-American Studies*. She has traveled the U.S. and Canada, training teachers, school leaders, and teacher education faculty.

She is the founder of Girls Got LIFE, a nonprofit organization that provides mentoring and leadership development for young girls.

www.drcathyo.com

www.edueffectiveness.com

Using PLCs to Solve School Problems

By Dr. Cathy Owens-Oliver

I n the education field, we have made the term PLC, or professional learning community, the new label for any small group of teachers working toward any common goal. But it's not a specific group, topic, or objective that constitutes a PLC. Every school is, in and of itself, a professional learning community, or it should be. The entire school community of educators, including non-instructional staff, are critical voices in the discussion on student achievement. Every voice matters in a professional learning community.

Effective PLC's must be comprised of teacher leaders, school principals, and others on staff who work collaboratively to solve school problems inside, out. No one knows a school better than those who work there every day. The people in the building (and online) are the ones who must take ownership of problems and be willing to work together to find or create solutions. They must focus on not only developing a school improvement plan but also determining which specific actions are necessary to implement the plan and bring it into reality. Effective schoolwide collaboration is how PLCs fill in the blanks between where their school is and where they want it to be.

To create a structure for this kind of collaborative planning, principals must be able to generate buy-in from the staff. Generating buy-in is a critical step toward demonstrating instructional leadership. Leaders must take deliberate actions to ensure that all teachers have a voice in the purpose and focus of PLCs, are able to engage in professional learning on a regular basis and will be able to generate evidence that their ongoing professional development transfers to classroom practice.

Buy-in for change always begins with a conversation. It's that simple. Principals must start the conversation with a vision for what can be, not a lecture on how bad things are and then provide a collaborative structure for schoolwide engagement. They must engage a team of strategic thinking gap closers who can assess the challenges in student learning, recommend approaches to address them, create a workable plan, and then work with peers to make it happen.

As instructional leaders, principals must demonstrate knowledge and skill in adult learning theory, relationship building, and emotional intelligence to successfully engage their full staff. Schools are naturally siloed; many on staff never get a chance of having a reason to work together. But every school principal must be intentional about pulling everyone together for meaningful, outcome-based dialogue. They must be willing to ask the provocative questions that make teachers look in the academic mirror at their own instructional performance. This leads to new practices and protocols for school improvement.

Implementation becomes real and change becomes evident when visionary principals give teacher leaders some autonomy, encourage their instructional decision making, and build a collaborative work environment teachers will thrive in and appreciate. Principals who share leadership opportunities give teachers a voice by demonstrating that in a learning community, every voice must be heard and considered, not just the one that is loudest.

Principals will see more consistent gains in student achievement when, rather than allowing problems to accumulate on their desk, they share them with teachers who lead. Teachers can assume shared responsibility for analyzing and addressing students' performance as well as providing their peers with a menu of tools and resources to improve instruction. Collaborating this way pushes teacher leaders to do more and helps them develop the skills to become even more effective.

But the administrator must set the tone for these conditions through activities and research-based strategies for engaging all teachers in professional learning experiences that will yield student learning gains. When PLCs are directly connected to what's happening across the school building and in individual classrooms, the new learning more quickly transfers into lesson implementation. Teachers must see themselves as the most powerful influencers of learning, and share their classroom wins with others on staff. Together, become empowered to lead schoolwide improvement programs.

The buy-in conversation is about what all staff in a PLC can do to design a teaching and learning culture that yields increased performance for teachers as well as students. Changing school culture starts with cross-collaboration among the entire teaching staff, including those who may be afraid of change or not yet equipped for it. Teachers and noninstructional staff need to see PLCs as not just another task to complete, but a direct strategy for elevating the skills and knowledge of everyone involved.

As I travel across the country, the feedback I hear from teachers is always the same. "We don't need business world experts who have never taught in K-12, to come in trying to fix us or our problems." I concur because educators who have worked in schools are the best *academic first responders*. I have always questioned how managers from corporate America, who don't know and haven't done the hard work and heart work of the classroom, can offer the best practical, effective decisions. Business expertise helps with technical management of how we do school, but instructional leadership must be underpinned with first-hand classroom knowledge.

Most of the problems schools face are best solved by teachers who deal with them head on every day. But while teachers may feel as though they don't need an outside expert, principals do need a facilitator or coach to help them create a structure and culture where possible solutions can be explored together and implemented fully. So, the buy-in conversation is not an informal chat loaded with personal and unrelated opinions as to how one would run the school differently. Instead, it is a candid, critical, and courageous conversation about what all staff can do to redesign the learning culture.

The principal must take the lead in placing high-stakes issues on the table for discussion and encourage teachers, as lead stakeholders, to speak up about why things are the way they are, how things can change, what solutions are possible, and what the next steps are for turning possibilities into reality. Principles who are true instructional leaders know the real value of PLCs is the ideation that comes from both large and small school improvement inquiry teams. There must be specific objectives evaluated by measurable outcomes. The outcomes are determined by changes in instructional practice.

Effective teaching is key to meeting the needs of all students, especially struggling learners. So, the PLCs must place targeted emphasis on better teaching to ensure better learning. Central to discussions of effective instructional practice of teachers, both individually and collectively, are the following topics:

1. Why and where are instructional changes needed?

2. What effective, research-based, instructional strategies will improve student learning and influence these changes?

3. What peer planning and teaching models do we need to ensure these strategies are learned and demonstrated effectively?

Teachers must be able to ask the hard questions, grapple with difficult answers, and do the hard work and the *heart work* necessary for affecting change. Again, principals must ensure the teachers and other staff feel a sense of ownership of school problems and have a safe, collaborative environment in which to work toward solutions. As a PLC, school and teacher leaders must value each other's voices in establishing end goals and determining a plan of action for reaching them.

You will see school change starting to take shape when teachers are empowered to lead school improvement. As I work with schools and districts, I make sure these five questions are included in buy-in conversations:

1. How do teachers at your school "own" some of the reasons for a student's low performance?

2. Do teachers have a shared understanding of what effective teaching looks like?

3. Do you see consistency in classroom expectations and instructional practices from one classroom to the next?

4. To what extent does your staff have the instructional knowledge necessary to teach 21st-century skills?

5. Does the school staff share a common language that makes communicating with parents and students easier?

The time to embrace instructional leaders and other teacher leaders is now. Post pandemic, the outside-in approach will not work. The idea is not to bring in another program. PLCs must be shaped around what is best for a specific group of students based on their individual needs. Literacy, social-emotional learning, math and science, technology, health and wellness, the arts, and all other subject matter now demands more effective teachers than ever before. They need to design lessons and deliver tailored instruction better than ever before. PLCs need to be more targeted and relevant than ever before.

Principals must generate buy-in for schoolwide change that engages both the teaching staff and the noninstructional staff. PLCs need to look and feel different as all educators, including some parents, gather to focus on how to get schools back on track and excited about learning. Teachers don't need to be told what to do. They need PLC meetings where they are encouraged and empowered to tell each other how they do what they do and get feedback on what tweaks to make when something isn't working. Think-pair-share is for them as well as their students. School leaders need to take a step back and give teachers who know what to do the space to run the plays they feel will change the game and get more wins for more students.

Hosea 4:6

Made in the USA
Columbia, SC
15 October 2021